Organisation and
Scientific Discovery

Organisation and Scientific Discovery

John Hurley
Dublin City University, Ireland

JOHN WILEY & SONS

Chichester · New York · Brisbane · Toronto · Singapore

Other Wiley Editorial Offices

John Wiley & Sons, Inc., 605 Third Avenue,
New York, NY 10158-0012, USA

Jacaranda Wiley Ltd, 33 Park Road, Milton,
Queensland 4064, Australia

John Wiley & Sons (Canada) Ltd, 22 Worcester Road,
Rexdale, Ontario M9W 1L1, Canada

John Wiley & Sons (Asia) Pte Ltd, Clementi Loop #02-01,
Jin Xing Distripark, Singapore 129809

Library of Congress Cataloging-in-Publication Data

Hurley, John.
    Organisation and scientific discovery / John Hurley
        p.   cm.
    Includes bibliographical references and index.
    ISBN 0-471-96963-X (cloth : alk. paper)
    1. Discoveries in science. 2. Organization. 3. Science–
–Methodology.   I. Title.
Q180.55 D57H87   1996
507'2—dc20   96-25877
                                                  CIP

British Library Cataloguing in Publication Data

A catalogue record for this book is available from the British Library

ISBN 0 471 96963 X

Typeset in 10 on 12pt Times by Dobbie Typesetting, Tavistock, Devon
Printed and bound in Great Britain by Biddles Ltd, Guildford, Surrey
This book is printed on acid-free paper responsibly manufactured from sustainable forestation,
for which at least two trees are planted for each one used for paper production

Contents

Preface

ON THE TRAIL OF DISCOVERY

This book addresses the question of how scientific research is most effectively organised in order to best facilitate creativity and discovery in science. It is written because the possibility that organisation may have an important influence on science research, and discovery in particular, has been largely ignored.

In the case of discovery, the outcome is so unique that it is by definition unknown—at least in any precise way. *Organisation* may well be needed, because the discoverer-scientist needs resources. Those resources are not simply money—though money is a useful shorthand term—but also the support of exceptional colleagues, technicians, library and equipment.

In order to extend our knowledge of the organisational factors related to discovery, it was decided to seek the collaboration of a number of Nobel laureates in the physical sciences. This book is an attempt to look at the level of the laboratory and its immediate environment, to see if organisational effects exist also. It was decided to approach scientists of proven ability in discovery (the Nobel laureates) rather than scientists in general, as it was felt that the scientist of proven creative capacity might have qualitatively different views from other scientists. All one hundred and sixty living Nobel laureates in the physical sciences were invited to participate; sixteen agreed.

Methodology

To explore the hypothesis that organisational factors may be important in relation to discovery, this study began by exploring the possible correlates of discovery, with scientists who had been shown to be significant discoverers: the Nobel laureates. This was done by carrying out two interviews with each Nobel laureate: an unstructured one and a structured one. Following the interviews, four questionnaires were administered to each scientist on the selection method used for the Nobel laureates, current selection practice, freedom and chance. Significant quotations from each interview, and the results of the questionnaires, are given in the text in the appropriate chapters.

The following is an overview of the topics that were consistently raised by the Nobel laureates as important for discovery:

1. Differing methods and approaches to scientific research
2. Freedom to think and experiment
3. Chance factors
4. Organisational factors (including resources, the selection of colleagues, the preparation of young scientists, supervision, technical support, etc.)

These aspects of discovery emphasised by the Nobel laureates have led to the development of a tentative organisational theory of discovery. The structure is quite divergent from the literature in this area, which tends to concentrate on individual creativity, on chance factors, on computational approaches or on sociological influences.

A model began to emerge during my discussions with the sixteen Nobel laureates. All of these scientists were of the view that novel ideas developed in their own minds, but all were very aware too, of the important role played by their favourable location in a well-resourced organisation. My own observation of the situation in which they worked led me to the view that to attribute the development of these ideas entirely to the individual would be to miss the subtler reality of the discovery process. Certainly the tentative final form of the discovery emerged in each individual's mind. However, unlike many scientists, the people I interviewed had the following:

1. All joined exceptionally well-resourced laboratories at an early stage.
2. All were supervised by scientists of exceptional talent early on.
3. All experienced organisational support which gave them great freedom and time to give rein to their own exceptional motivation.
4. All worked in laboratories which allowed them to capitalise on chance.
5. All worked in well developed laboratories.
6. All had immense personal leadership and organisation characteristics.

These observations have led me to suggest a strong organisational role in the discovery process, which, while acknowledging the central contribution of individual factors to discovery, provides an elaboration of our understanding of the wider range of processes, chiefly organisational ones.

However, our discoverer-scientists must be endowed also with clarity of vision in their scientific fields, and dedication and persistence in pursuit of their goals, coupled with exceptional skill in organising, leading and creating enthusiasm. This hypothesis is more difficult to prove. Certainly we can look at the success of their experimentation and their obvious discovery, and say *post hoc* that they have these abilities. It would, however, be even more useful if we could identify these capacities at the point of selection of the young scientist.

The book also summarises much of what is known in a specifically *organisational* context. One of the reasons why research into organisational processes related to discovery has been very sparse may be the wide acceptance of the role of chance or serendipity in discovery. The view seems to be: 'if chance factors are important, then no matter how well we organise, how can that help?' However, as we know, chance is inclined to favour the efforts of those who are well prepared for it. There has been a fascination with the 'chance' aspect of Pasteur's view of discovery and a certain marked avoidance of the 'preparation' aspect. In a similar way, Edison's famous remark that 'invention is 1% inspiration, 99% perspiration' the perspiration aspect of which has also been ignored. The emphasis that has been placed on 'inspiration' in creativity research, for example, far exceeds the attention given to 'perspiration', including the preparation of the scientist. Much of that preparation takes place at the level of the organisational provision of resources and the selection and development of staff; hence it would seem that good scientific organisation can only enhance any possible chance effects.

This book reports a qualitative study, exploring the role of organisation in scientific discovery. It makes no claim to being based on a representative sample of eminent scientists; clearly the numbers involved are too small for that. Nevertheless, the book has a number of unique aspects to it: it is based on a group of scientists who have made substantial discoveries; it is oriented to the role of organisation in scientific research; it takes issue with the individual psychology of research, the cult of the 'epic hero'; it points to a very substantial area of future research, which may be of great use to scientific discovery; and it points to the almost total lack of a theoretical base for the organisation of research.

Much of what we understand as 'organisation theory' refers to the processes and structures in very large organisations with very little in common with either scientific research groups or even with scientific organisations. The traditional industrial or bureaucratic organisation structure is geared in the main towards organisational processes which are directed to producing standard goods or services.

There is a need to construct a significant and relevant model of the functioning of research organisations and groups, and to formulate a theory to explain important relationships. This is needed principally because one does not exist but a theoretical framework is also needed to guide experimental research to test the theory and to establish the parameters of organisation in relation to discovery.

Those responsible for research projects, both large and small, have no models, traditions, guidelines or textbooks to help them structure and manage their exploration. Most existing textbooks, models and theories are in fact based in our industrial past and on examples of organisation taken in the main from traditional models such as the army, the church, the bureaucracy and the manufacturing plant. These organisations all exist in order to ensure that activities are carried out in a standardised way, and seem quite inappropriate, and even inimical, to the organisation of exploratory scientific research, the aim of which is to produce novel and unique solutions to scientific problems.

In the chapters that follow, an attempt is made to build on what the Nobel laureates tell us is important in discovery-oriented science and to argue for an organisational theory and practice that will support research and increase the probability of discovery. There is no suggestion of producing a formula, a causal model of discovery; this may well be logically impossible. Nevertheless, if a convincing argument is presented which will show that discovery can be made more likely, given certain organisational factors, this could make an important contribution to the quality of subsequent research.

Why choose the Nobel prize as a measure of scientific effectiveness?

This research was directed from the beginning to exploring the organisational situation in which discovery occurs in science. The choice of Nobel laureates as exemplars is not without flaws. One is relying very heavily on the judgement of one committee — however prestigious. However, any criterion of creativity in science is subject to argument. This one was chosen because, though there is disagreement on those people who have been disregarded for Nobel prizes, there is significant support within the scientific community for the validity of those chosen.

The Nobel Prize is the most prestigious prize in science that exists. According to Cole and Cole (1967) it is the most visible and widely accepted award. Furthermore, Cole and Cole carried out a study to relate the Nobel prizewinners' other achievements, in particular their publications. Nobel laureates had on average 58 publications, compared to an average of 5.5 publications for other scientists.

Cole and Cole (1973) conceive of a hierarchy of scientific excellence as follows:

> At the apex of this hierarchy we find . . . originators of new paradigms like Einstein or Planck, or great geniuses like Bohr, Fermi and Pauling. Right below this handful of geniuses are the brilliant scientists who have been awarded the most coveted of scientific honours, such as the Nobel prize, or election to various national academies of science . . . they total no more than a few thousand out of one million active scientists in the world.

Cole and Cole were writing nearly twenty years ago. There are now around five million scientists, but very few of these are involved in significant discovery. Cole and Cole continue:

> The mass of scientists, even those who spend some time on research, are remarkably unproductive. They produce few ideas and rarely put anything in print. Although these scientists remain relatively invisible to the larger scientific community, they may well have achieved prestige as excellent teachers of science, or as the ranking members of their college or university science department.

For these reasons the choice of Nobel laureates as examples of scientists involved in discovery seems a reasonable one.

Structure of the book

The book is constructed in two parts. In the first part, the dynamics of discovery, including the role of method, chance, freedom and philosophy are explored. The second part details the possible role of organisation in relation to the foregoing, and as an important factor in increasing the probability of discovery. It outlines the main organisational processes involved in discovery, including the process of joining a scientific organisation, group processes in science, the management of science, rewards systems and individual and organisational development.

The final chapter is an attempt to bring the findings of this research together and to suggest the way in which the new theoretical framework relating discovery with organisation, which is proposed here, might be tested.

Acknowledgements

I would like to acknowledge firstly my debt of gratitude to the Nobel laureates for agreeing to be interviewed by me and for their enthusiastic involvement, including completing the four questionnaires in relation to this study. Without their involvement this study would lack a vital element: the views and experiences of recognised discoverer-scientists. I was honoured to meet them, and hope this work will justify their faith in me.

I would like to acknowledge the extensive help and encouragement of a number of other people, significant to the process of this study. The project began in Dublin City University over a lunch-time walk with Chris Curran. His many ideas and insights have been most valuable to me in relation to this project, as was his encouragement when things looked very difficult to achieve.

Also in DCU, I was advised in relation to scientific matters by Eugene Kennedy, Richard O'Kennedy and Albert Pratt; they and their colleagues, Rosaline Devery, John Gallagher, Joshua Howarth and Robert Forster, helped bring up to date the brief biographical notes on the Nobel laureates involved in this study.

Charles McCorkell was very helpful in developing ideas as to how to illustrate the process of discovery in graphic form. I am grateful, too, for the many discussions, suggestions and criticisms made by my colleagues Finian Buckley, Peter Chisnall, Tony Moynihan and Jim Whyte. I also appreciate the suggestions from very many colleagues in the Business School and in particular, the very positive support I received from the Dean, Anthony Walsh.

The librarians at both DCU and Stanford were enormously helpful in locating elusive texts, and I appreciate this assistance very much.

I would also like to acknowledge the work of John McCann, a graduate of our degree course on Organisational Psychology, for his critical reading of a late draft and for his work in relation to the creativity literature which has made a very useful contribution to Chapter 2.

In Stanford University, I am very grateful to Dick Snow, the Professor of Education, for his hospitality and help in all aspects of my stay at Stanford, and to Jim March of Scancor for his many discussions and for reading an early draft of this book. I am also grateful to Dick Clark in the University of

Southern California for his help and encouragement in spending a period in the United States. I would like to acknowledge, too, my appreciation of the support of the Fulbright Commission for funding part of my stay in America and of the British Council for its funding of my interviews of the British scientists. In Stanford, too, I would like to acknowledge the work of Janet Stemwedel in relation to the Nobel laureates' biographies and to the development of certain sections on the experience of scientists in different laboratories.

I also spent a brief period working on this book project in the University of Nijmegen, in the Netherlands. I would like to acknowledge the welcome and support I received in Nijmegen, particularly from my good friend, Charles de Wolff.

My family and friends have been immensely supportive of this project. My wife Elizabeth has been very helpful with editorial criticism which has been much needed. My eldest daughter Justine did valuable work in relation to the extraction of quotable sections of the Nobel laureates' interviews. My son Stephen with his background in science was invaluable in reading certain articles and picking out cogent points from them, and my younger daughter Sara carried out valuable checking work in relation to the final references. For all their work and support over the years, many thanks. My good friends, John Murphy, Dermot Kehoe, Dermot Egan, Cormac Keane, Eugene O'Sullivan and Martin Maher, have provided a useful foil for discussions of the strategic nature of the scientific enterprise.

J.H.

Chapter 1

Discovery and Organisation in Science

1 INTRODUCTION

Discovery is one of the most fascinating events in the human experience. To a scientist, the joy of discovering something until then unknown is like the experience of Columbus making his landfall in the Americas. Like Columbus, the scientist must make a journey into the unknown and uncharted in the hope of making a discovery, yet not sure what that discovery will be. Discovery, whether planned or unplanned, is always hoped for and laboriously pursued. It is often not quite what was expected and is frequently unanticipated in form and detail. Nature is reluctant to give up her secrets, and unfolds an often different unrevealed dimension. Discovery, then, comes as a surprise. It represents an unanticipated unfolding of a hitherto unknown aspect of the natural world.

The purpose of this book is to subject our individual-oriented view of discovery to a re-examination. The way we conceive of discovery has strong effects not only on the way science is organised but also on the way scientists are selected, supervised, trained and developed. Furthermore, our views have an effect on the research we carry out, on the processes involved in discovery and on the allocation of resources to such research. The book is also written because there is a real possibility that many influences other than those commonly credited with this role have an important effect on scientific research, and in particular on discovery.

In order to extend our knowledge of the many factors related to discovery, it was decided to seek the collaboration of a number of Nobel laureates in the physical sciences. All of these individuals are acknowledged to have made significant discoveries and theoretical contributions to their field. This book considers science at the level of the laboratory and its immediate environment and attempts to identify, in an exploratory way, those organisational factors most central to the occurrence of discovery in scientific projects.

This study was stimulated by a number of separate insights. Research by the author into the effects of technology on work made contact with science projects and led to an understanding of the unique nature of the scientific organisation. Strangely, however, no research appeared to exist on the organisation dimension of science using discovery as a criterion. This seemed very strange since science laboratories are models of a very special kind of organisation, certainly worthy of more than a casual interest.

It was also observed that scientific discovery appeared to take place in very few institutions, which would suggest the influence of an organisational resource-related dimension. Taking this into account, one begins to wonder whether the nature of organisation could be a significant factor in discovery.

It was these insights and observations that prompted a comprehensive search through the literature for studies relating discovery with organisation. Some literature appeared to cover this area, and titles existed which suggested it did. On closer examination, however, it was found that these authors did not cover precisely the relationship between discovery and organisation. Often the focus was on some very specific aspect of the process of discovery such as problem-solving, or logic or computation. Examples of such texts include Nickles (1978), Langley (1987), Shrager and Langley (1990) and Lamb (1991).

Other literature refers to innovation in organisations, by which is meant organisational changes, role and task innovations; innovations in management and leadership practices. Examples of such texts are: Zaltman, Duncan and Holbeck (1973), Davis and Cherns (1975) and Amabile (1983) In these texts the focus of the innovation is the organisation itself, and the organisations are often large manufacturing companies or service providers. The focus is not usually on the outcomes of organisational processes, rather on the organisational processes themselves.

Some texts have focused on scientific outcomes. *Scientists in Organisations* by Pelz and Andrews (1976) is a comprehensive study. The book speaks about differing levels of creativity, but not about discovery. In addition, the scientists in this study worked in a large scientific bureaucracy, and were not necessarily discoverers. In any case, Pelz and Andrews did not find any relationship between creativity and their scientists' outputs or technical performance.

One study by a physicist is particularly interesting. *Discovering* by Root-Bernstein (1989) is a scientist's attempt to explore how discovery is affected by other factors. Root-Bernstein does indeed reach quite substantial conclusions as to the multiple causes of discovery and argues quite convincingly against the solitary genius school of thought. However, though this book implies a strong role for organisation in relation to discovery, it does not make this role explicit, except, perhaps, in a passing reference to organisation in a diagram.

On the other hand, a large general literature on creativity does exist. This area of research, some of which relates to science, has one rather significant drawback. It seems to take it as given that creativity is necessarily equated with discovery. Pervading this literature is the idea that the creative genius makes discoveries and that one can measure creativity by means of tests. Implied, too, is the view that we can predict discovery by testing scientists.

The idea that geniuses make discoveries has a certain ring of circularity about it: a scientist is a scientist until he or she makes a discovery of note; then he or she is a genius. The trouble with this idea, apart from the logical problem, is that it is a counsel of despair; we can do nothing about it. We must simply wait until the next discovery is made and then announce the overnight birth of a new genius. We cannot identify or select such people, we cannot train them and we cannot figure out how to manage them, because we cannot identify them until they have made a discovery.

Although the idea that the creative genius makes discoveries has some intuitive appeal, it may be an inadequate explanation of reality. There are many examples of individuals who are full of rather brilliant ideas, but who lack the persistence or continued interest to follow up their ideas with the necessary amount of hard work to bring them to possible fruition. It may be a more reasonable assumption that, like the variation that exists in intelligence, similar variation exists in levels of creativity among all individuals. Certain generally available basal levels of creativity are needed in scientists in order for them to make discoveries, but that this is by no means the deciding factor in discovery.

Creativity as distinct from genius, however, might well be a more hopeful field. If creativity were related to discovery, then if we could measure creativity and devise valid tests to identify it, we could use these tests to select scientists who might have a better chance of being discoverers. This link has never been studied in those scientists who are agreed to be discoverers; it has simply been assumed.

A similar point can be made about accidental or chance occurrences. Chance may well exist as a sort of background to all scientific activity, but it is the observation and use of chance factors that are important, not the existence of chance itself. In any case, we cannot actually do anything about it except wait until someone, by making good use of chance occurrences, is deemed to be lucky. No conclusions for selection or organisation can be drawn.

Is it not likely that discovery in science depends on both individual and organisational factors? The individual discoverer-scientist is likely to be highly interested in science, of high intelligence and strongly motivated to get to the bottom of at least some research problems. However, it is also true that, whether by selection or attraction, this scientist will work in a well-resourced organisation, be it a university, research institute or commercial laboratory. In addition, this scientist will have considerable ability at organising research and leading colleagues, over and above his or her specifically scientific ability.

Is it not likely, too, that the organisation of a discovery-oriented laboratory will be very different from an organisation oriented to a defined product? The desired outcome of such a laboratory is discovery — a totally unique and non-standard outcome. The organisation may, in its appearance, look similar to that surrounding a regular standard product, but the dynamics of its processes will be experienced very differently by its principal actors. In the case of an organisation devoted to the production of a standard product or service, the organisation centres around the assurance of quality and standardisation. This implies the establishment of rigorous standards and routines, and the careful checking and monitoring of all activities connected to them. Control and conformity are emphasised, and individuals operate within very narrow clearly stated guidelines. Control of all activities operates through a hierarchically distributed chain of command.

Where the desired outcome is discovery, though the laboratory may be situated within a larger hierarchical control framework, be it a university, institute or commercial enterprise, that laboratory will be characterised by freedom above all — not absolute freedom, and not endless time and boundless resources, but freedom above all to use one's own personality in pursuit of a scientific objective, freedom to pursue hunches down possibly pointless avenues of exploration and freedom to theorize, experiment, accept, or reject, according to the principal investigator's own judgement, with no other interference.

Considerable organisational resources are needed to allow this freedom and give the principal investigator time to reach a satisfactory conclusion. Resources are not simply money, though inevitably money is a shorthand for many other resources, but key resources include above all the support of exceptional colleagues. What organisational hierarchy does exist within the laboratory is in place not to control, but to support, the scientists' work. The principal investigator may often be quite junior, and yet be in charge of his or her project. The more senior people in the laboratory, in particular the research director, may have the function of supporting the more junior person, in a way that is the opposite of that pertaining in an organisation turning out a routine product.

How could it be otherwise? To turn out discoveries in pre-planned mechanised batches is not the nature of discovery.

We need to know considerably more about what organisational processes precede discovery. We know a lot about how many individual scientists think from their published work and their achievements. These usually address the problem at issue and are expressed in abstract, impersonal, terms. The processes of science thus often appear to be solitary matters, and in the case of some scientists they *are* solitary matters. In most science, the completion of the final clarifications of their contributions is also quite solitary. Yet science is actually a very social enterprise, involving groups of people working around a problem, particularly at the experimental phase. Here the principal investigator is surrounded by colleagues, assistants and technicians operating as an *ad hoc* team closing in on a shared problem. In the earlier problem identification and hypothesis generation phases, argument and discussion of a formal and informal nature takes place. The related literature is discussed and anomalies and incompleteness are acknowledged. Sacred cows are ritually dismissed. All of this is obviously a group process and takes place furthermore in an organisational context. This context is the subject of the present study.

2 THE ROLE OF ORGANISATION IN RELATION TO DISCOVERY

The sheer magnitude of research and descriptive material on the role of the individual in science and discovery may have obscured a central fact: that it occurs only in certain parts of the world and only then in certain laboratories. Eigen (1991) cites an example of this phenomenon by highlighting the distribution of eminent scientists throughout the world. The results are shown in Table 1.

Within Germany these prizewinners were located in only four universities; Berlin, Gottingen, Heidelberg and Munich. In the United Kingdom these prizewinners were located in only three centres: Cambridge, Oxford and London. In the rest of Europe, France had 6, Switzerland 4, Scandinavia 7, Benelux 2. In the United States the prizewinners were in six locations in the following order: Harvard, Princeton, New York, Stanford, Berkeley and Pasadena. (See also Zuckermann (1977) for an earlier study, the results of which show the same general distribution.)

When three countries in the world provide most of all known prizewinners and all the other countries only one quarter, one is bound to consider that there is some characteristic of those countries' educational and cultural systems that in some way fosters creative discovery more than others. Likewise, within those cultures it is clear that only a few laboratories have been successful in these terms. This latter fact suggests an organisational effect, rather than a sociocultural one. Taking the more recent figures from *The Nobel Foundation Directory, 1995–1996*, using only those laureates now living, we see a similar pattern of the distribution of Nobel awards (Table 2).

One can see from these figures the extraordinary domination of Europe and the United States, for which there are a number of possible explanations. For example, the differences could be due to the availability of resources, societal differences, differing orientations towards free thought or differences in the

Table 1 Location of Nobel prizewinners in Chemistry 1901–1983 (Eigen, 1991)

Location	Germany	UK	USA	Rest of the world
Numbers	25	23	27	26

Table 2 Distribution of living Nobel laureates 1994 (*The Nobel Foundation Directory, 1995–1996*)

Total	Europe	USA	Rest of the world
166	102	59	5

basic teaching and preparation of scientists. Another point worth noting is that in addition to the relative absence of awards in the rest of the world, there is a corresponding absence within those countries of awards in Europe and the United States to scientists in most universities, labs and institutes. This is not surprising in view of the enormous differences in the resources, including the quality of academic staff, that exist throughout these sectors. In many top universities, not only are resources in terms of library stock, access to information and funding very great, but also the calibre of many of the scientists' colleagues is truly exceptional. At the other end of the university spectrum there are those institutions where the emphasis is on teaching as opposed to research, and with insufficient resources of the kind listed in Chapter 4. In addition, most of the teaching staff may not have many publications or may not have been educated to PhD level. There are certainly gradations of universities on this spectrum, between these two extremes. However, organisational support for excellence in research is absent in the vast majority.

Within the group of those institutions where research resources are limited, only a small number of Nobel laureates or other eminent scientists exist. It is clear that most awards have been made to scientists in top universities, which are well resourced, have exceptional library stock and numerous eminent colleagues. The research institutes are all well funded and closely linked with top universities. Awards made in commercial labs are relatively few in number, though most of these are well funded and resourced. One could argue that university organisation and climate is more encouraging of discovery-oriented thinking than commercial labs. This is because of the commercial laboratories' understandable orientation to the development and exploitation of discoveries rather than to discovery itself.

Table 3 shows the distribution of Nobel prizes by type of institution and shows that by far the greatest number were awarded in universities and research institutes.

Table 3 Distribution of Nobel laureates by type of institution (1994) (*The Nobel Foundation Directory, 1995–1996*)

All	University	Research institute	Commercial laboratory
166	100	48	18

When we consider that natural scientific talent is likely to be equally distributed throughout the world, yet discovery takes place in only a very few laboratories, it seems reasonable to suggest that organisational factors play an important, and perhaps decisive, role in discovery. Yet since the presentation by Guilford in 1950 (Guilford, 1956), there has been considerable interest in creativity as an individual characteristic. Extensive research has concentrated on the measurement of creativity in individuals. The relationship between measured creativity in individual scientists, with significant discovery on their part, has never been explored. As mentioned earlier, it appears to be assumed in the creativity research that scientists who are measurably more creative will discover more frequently than those who are less so. The interaction of other personality variables, notably persistence (Edison's 99% perspiration), curiosity and hard work, have not been explored. The effects of working in particular organisational environments has also never been studied.

If we begin to see a case emerging for the importance of organisation in relation to discovery, then perhaps our emphasis on the role of the individual in the past has been too restrictive. It is possible that the case for a greater recognition of the importance of the role of the organisation in relation to discovery needs to be made more explicit.

3   WHY IS SCIENTIFIC DISCOVERY SO IMPORTANT?

Scientific discovery is important in a number of different ways. It is considered important because of its scale, the large number of scientists working in research, the contribution to the global economy, in its contributions to our standard of living and in its potential to solve many of our problems. As a result of scientific discovery, we have seen dramatic improvements in public health, in such areas as the decline in childhood mortality and increased lifespan. Productivity increases have taken place in agriculture and many other fields as a result of the application of scientific research. Furthermore, discovery opens up new potential areas of improvement, without which we could not dream of continuing general increases in our standard of living.

Max Perutz (1989) documents the contribution of science to our world very well, and in particular identifies the key contributions science has made in the areas of food production, health and energy. Briefly, Perutz demonstrated that in the years from 1950 to 1971, food production doubled, in health, life expectancy has been greatly extended and in energy science has provided a variety of new means of energy production to replace non-renewable resources.

Many exciting new challenges exist at the frontiers of science today. For instance, Scott (1990) has brought together fourteen examples of these developing areas, including the possibility of artificial photosynthesis and the production of electricity from microbes.

The development, and even the continuance, of our civilisation depends on genuinely creative scientific research. We are faced with immense challenges and with difficult but solvable problems for science. Yet the organisation and training and development of those involved in scientific research appears to be organised in a way that depends little on the expertise available in the organisational domain and more on the way things have been done in the past.

At the same time, some developments in science pose threats to our environment, by way of radiation, food-chain damage, global warming, species extinction and many others.

4 THE HUMAN AND FINANCIAL SCALE OF SCIENCE RESEARCH

World-wide, large numbers of individuals are involved in scientific research as a full-time profession. According to UNESCO (1993) the following numbers of scientists and engineers work in science:

Year	Numbers
1980	3 920 754
1985	4 402 754
1990	5 223 614

Expenditure on scientific research is also substantial:

Year	Expenditure
1980	$208 370 000 000
1985	$271 850 000 000
1990	$452 590 000 000

These figures show two trends: the number of scientists in research is increasing and expenditure is also increasing. However, they do not show the full picture. Such is the scale of modern science that it is now a substantial part of world and national GDP. The figures given above are only for those directly involved in science research. Yet there is hardly any aspect of the world we live in that is not directly affected by discoveries of the recent past. In fact, when the laser was invented, hardly any use could be put forward for it. Now, laser surgery is routine and CD-based computer packages and entertainment are a large part of our daily life.

Given the significance of the field, the importance that we place on the organisation of science research cannot be overestimated. In order to be able to evaluate the contribution of organisations to discovery, it is important that we can develop an adequate definition of it, in order that it can be measured. Otherwise almost any scientific activity can be considered to be discovery.

5 WHAT IS DISCOVERY?

Discovery in one form or another happens all the time. When a child learns a new word, that is discovery for him. When a new skill is learned or area of knowledge is opened up, that is discovery. It is therefore important that we distinguish between discovery for the individual and discovery that adds to the sum of human knowledge. One very important characteristic of discovery is novelty. In science many discoveries are made on a daily basis. They all add something to the sum of human knowledge, though most discoveries are the honing down of some technique or the refinement of some process, the general principles of which are already known. Clarifications are also made that add to our detailed understanding of theory.

Most scientists hope that by hard work or by luck they may come to some discovery which is both new and of substantial importance. Scientists work away in the hope that they may discover something which makes a really substantial impact on our lives. They do this within a scientific framework and method.

Discovery in science, however, is not easy to define. It could be argued that discovery is discontinuous from other scientific research, in a plane totally beyond the achievements of other scientists. It could also be argued that it is an extreme point on a continuum, but still related to other scientific work, and part of the general scientific effort. There is no agreement on these two positions, and this is part of the problem in defining discovery.

At one level, all those who have completed doctorates may be regarded as having made some sort of discovery, because of the requirement for novelty in a PhD dissertation. However, most of these discoveries may never contribute substantially to science, yet logically they must be described as discoveries. In the case of major scientific advances, we have no difficulty in describing them as discoveries, but even major achievements fall into a number of different categories. Some discoveries are of the nature of reformulations and complete revisions of older paradigms. For example, the theory of relativity, as we know, had substantial implications on a variety of areas of science. Other discoveries, though clearly major advances, are more the result of persistent working out of difficult problems and need have no necessary implications for theoretical revision. Kantorovich (1993, p. 11) describes discovery in outcome terms:

> Discovery is a 'success' word. When we say we have discovered something, it means, for example, that the product of discovery is useful, that it solves a problem, explains some phenomena or that it is the lost object we have been looking for.

Discovery is defined in the *Oxford English Dictionary* as:

> To disclose or expose to view, anything covered up, hidden or previously unseen.
> To obtain sight or knowledge of something previously unknown, for the first time.
> To come to the knowledge of, to find out.

Interestingly, the encyclopedias of McGraw-Hill, *Chambers Dictionary of Science and Technology*, and van Nostrand's *Scientific Encyclopedia*, did not include any definition of discovery! This author proposes the following working definition of scientific discovery for consideration:

> Scientific discovery occurs when a scientific problem is solved; when a new technique is developed; when a more comprehensive theoretical explanation of existing phenomena is put forward; or when we come to the knowledge of new phenomena. Discovery means the addition of something new to the sum of human knowledge, and must be verifiable within a scientific framework.

This definition avoids the use of the words 'significant' and 'major'. Our current use of the word 'discovery', means in most cases 'significant discovery'. Therefore this definition is probably too wide and inclusive for an accurate measurement of the numbers of discoveries that take place. Yet it is always possible that some apparently minor discovery, at one time, may be seen as of major importance at a later date. Nevertheless, in the absence of a better definition, this one is proposed. Others will perhaps contribute to its precise development over time. An accurate and agreed definition of discovery is very important for future studies, which may attempt to quantify discovery by laboratory and to relate discovery to other possible variables.

Discovery involves developing new and creative insights, and testing these insights in scientific work. This is achieved by the construction of exquisitely designed experiments, carried out to test their performance under predetermined conditions. According to Lonergan (1957, page 4):

> Discovery is new beginning. It is the origin of new rules that supplement, or even supplant, the old. Genius is creative. It is genius precisely because it disregards established routines, because it originates the novelties that will be the routines of the future. Were there rules for discovery, then discoveries would be mere conclusions.

Discovery is open to examination, replication, dispute, discussion, falsification and verification in the public domain. Diderot (1753) described the scientific process:

> We have three principal means: observation of nature, reflection, and experiment. Observation gathers the facts, reflection combines them, experiment verifies the result of the combination. It is essential that the observation of nature be assiduous, that reflection be profound, and that experimentation be exact. Rarely does one see these abilities in combination. And so, creative geniuses are not common.

This view of the scientific process emphasises individual genius, yet strangely presents science as a somewhat more mechanical process than characterises most research. The period of reflection which Helmholz referred to in 1871 as 'incubation' represents a formative stage of a discovery (Wallas, 1926). However, though it is generally assumed that reflection takes place in the mind of the individual scientist alone, it may not be an adequate description of what actually happens. For those involved in most science research, the role of the group is important. Organisational factors can also have an important influence. For example, as a necessary part of the reflective process, the scientist must become immersed in the problem. This would involve education and training as well as the use of organisational resources such as library facilities. In addition, it will usually be necessary to discuss issues and problems with colleagues, the availability and competence of whom will vary depending on the organisation.

Reflection and insight develops, of course, within individuals. In reality, however, the whole process of discovery could be described more accurately (albeit less colourfully) as a group/organisational achievement. In other words, discovery is more likely to be the result of a gradual accumulation of knowledge and the combined input of the members of the research group. It seems, however, that the ideas of 'genius' and 'flashes of insight' are much more attractive as illustrations of scientific discovery than concepts such as 'persistence' and 'curiosity' and 'compendious knowledge'. Beveridge (1980, p. 34) puts it well:

> It is commonly believed that the act of discovery is a sudden event, arising either from a flash of intuition, or a serendipitous observation, or the outcome of one experiment. But in fact it is only the conception of new knowledge that occurs suddenly; usually this is followed by a long and often difficult gestation of confirmation and development, so that only gradually does the discovery come to maturity.

Kantarovich (1993) points to the gradual, often painstakingly slow, process which is research:

> Personally, a scientist may make very few scientific discoveries, if any during his lifetime; most scientific discoveries are products of collective efforts. Therefore, it is sometimes difficult to judge who participated in, or contributed to, the discovery; sometimes it is perhaps a whole community which should be credited. If the process extends over a long period of time, only the final step in the process is regarded as a discovery. Yet the contributions of the other participants are sometimes no less important than the contribution which constituted the breakthrough.

Clearly this description of the process of discovery is very different from the traditional 'instant illumination' that pervades the literature. It suggests, too, a considerable role for the group and for the organisation in which the group is embedded.

The physicist James Bryant Conant (1947) also saw science as a continuous process of development, progressing from one level of insight to another over the centuries. Polanyi (1962) also considered science research as constituting an 'invisible college' of scientists throughout the world and spread over time, who work together to get closer to their goal. An example of this gradual process involving the refinement of knowledge, which so characterises scientific research, is given by Galison (1987, p. 126):

> Eighteenth-Century natural philosophers noticed how electroscopes spontaneously lost their charge. Anachronistically one could say that these observers 'discovered' the muon since now physicists ascribe such discharges in large part to sea-level muons. With similar cogency some commentators have argued that Bothe and Kolhörster's counter coincidence experiments indicated the passage of particles that in retrospect we call muons. And, of course, there is a sense in which Carlson and Oppenheimer discovered the muon, since in 1936 they were the first to suggest (in print) the existence of a particle of intermediate mass as the penetrating component of cosmic radiation. Anderson and Neddermeyer first presented good data showing that energy-loss measurements of shower particles fitted the quantum theory. This implied — though again this can only be said in retrospect — that the penetrating particles must be other than electrons. Or Street and Stevenson could be credited with the discovery for having shown that there was a characteristic difference between the shower-producing power of shower particles and of penetrating particles.

He points out later:

> Instead of looking for a 'moment of discovery', we should envisage the ending of the muon experiments as a progressively refined articulation of a set of phenomena. In a sense the experiment had to end several times. At each stage of the process, a new characteristic could be ascribed to the cosmic rays: they discharged electroscopes; the discharge rate varied in a certain fashion with depth in matter; the shower particles were more easily absorbed than the single particles. In fact the final 'demonstration experiments' by Anderson, Neddermeyer, Street, and Stevenson rest their persuasive force on a great number of earlier experiments. Some of these efforts tested the apparatus such as when Street and Stevenson used the cloud chamber to certify the validity of the counter method against the AMNP attack. Other experiments served to forge a more direct link between theory and experiment. Such was the object of Fussell's cloud chambers with thin plates. He exhibited how the simple processes of pair production and bremsstrahlung underlay a phenomenon previously thought to be complex: showers.

These are examples of discovery as a gradual, long-term, process. Though many talented scientists were involved in the processes leading up to our present state of knowledge, it seems clear that without the continuity and support provided by organisational settings, much of this would not have been achieved.

This view of discovery reflected in Beveridge and in Kantarovich is gradually taking precedence over the flash of insight view or the traditional reference to chance factors as formative of discovery. This view — since it refers to a gradual process—implies a reliance on the wider scientific group as the context in which the individual scientist makes discoveries.

One of the most comprehensive studies of scientists in their organisations was carried out by Pelz and Andrews from 1951 to 1965, and reported in 1966. In this study, the scientist was viewed for the first time as a member of a group and of a wider organisation. Pelz and Andrews' work was useful in studying the actual work scientists do. Their key results were (1966, p. 7):

● Effective scientists were self-directed by their own ideas, and valued freedom. But at the same time they allowed other people a voice in shaping their directions; they interacted vigorously with colleagues.
● Effective scientists did not limit their activities either to the world of 'application' or to the world of 'pure science' but maintained an interest in both; their work was diversified.
● Effective scientists were not fully in agreement with their organisation in terms of their interests; what they personally enjoyed did not necessarily help them advance in the structure.
● Effective scientists tended to be motivated by the same kinds of things as their colleagues. At the same time, however, they differed from their colleagues in the styles and strategies with which they approached their work.
● Effective scientists did not limit their activities either to the world of 'application' or that of 'pure science' but maintained an interest in both; their work was diversified. Effective scientists were not fully in agreement with their organisation in terms of their interests; what they personally enjoyed did not necessarily help them in the structure.
● Effective scientists tended to be motivated by the same sort of things as their colleagues. At the same time, however, they differed from their colleagues in the styles and strategies with which they approached their work.

This study covered a wide range of topics and also attempted to measure creative output. In addition, it acknowledges the distinction between creativity as an ability and 'payoffs' from that ability. Pelz and Andrews (1966) found that the strongest factor affecting creative productivity was time spent in the particular area or topic. In other words, creative people usually had creative outputs if given sufficient time. Paradoxically, they also found that creative people were most useful to a project when they were new to it. Age did not have any effect here.

6 THE PROCESS OF DISCOVERY

There are probably as many reasons for scientists to work in research as there are scientists. Some may do it because they need a job, some because they see the potential contribution to mankind, some will become involved out of curiosity and some have an interest in the technology and processes involved. Hence there is room in science for many and diverse personalities, each attracted by differing aspects of science.

Interest began in the last century in the processes leading to discovery. Van Helmholz noted that a series of stages appeared to occur in the discovery process. Speaking at a banquet in 1871, he suggested three stages: preparation, incubation and illumination. Wallas (1926) added one more: verification. Subsequent research (see Boxenbaum, 1991) has suggested perhaps six stages, one coming before — interest — and one coming after — development. This model can be conceived as shown in Figure 1.

These stages are not themselves organisational processes, but more the metaphorical description of processes scientists usually go through. Nevertheless, as we shall see, they have substantial implications for the nature of the organisation of a scientific project. Figure 2 is an attempt to show the organisational implications of the Wallas model. Each of the stages described by Wallas have their associated activities, and consequent implications of an organisational nature.

In another attempt to describe the process of discovery, Conant (1947) outlines the process as shown in Figure 3. Conant gives the example of atomic theory to illustrate this, and describes the Greek atomist's ideas of nature as composed of ultimate particles as a speculative idea. It took a very long time for Dalton in 1800 to come up with a broad working hypothesis in relation to the atomic composition of simple elements and compounds, which he later developed into a conceptual scheme, after he had shown how fruitful his conceptual scheme was in chemical experiments.

Some psychological views of scientific discovery are either very close to explanations of learning, as in Hanson (see Brannigan, 1981). In this type of discovery, an individual may discover something which is new to that individual, and therefore a discovery for them, as, for example, when a child learns to read. This is not a discovery in our sense, and this theory may have only peripheral interest to discovery-related research.

An epistemological explanation may be given as was done by Blackwell. (Brannigan, 1981). Blackwell's model of discovery — which he based on an analysis of attempts by Newton and Descartes to formulate a law of inertia — is as follows:

(a) selection of relevant circumstances,
(b) the discrete specification of circumstances (Y if and only if X),
(c) the idealization of concepts (e.g., point mass, instantaneous velocity),

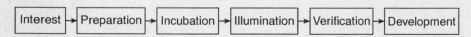

Figure 1   This process of scientific research (Van Helmholz–Wallas–Boxenbaum)

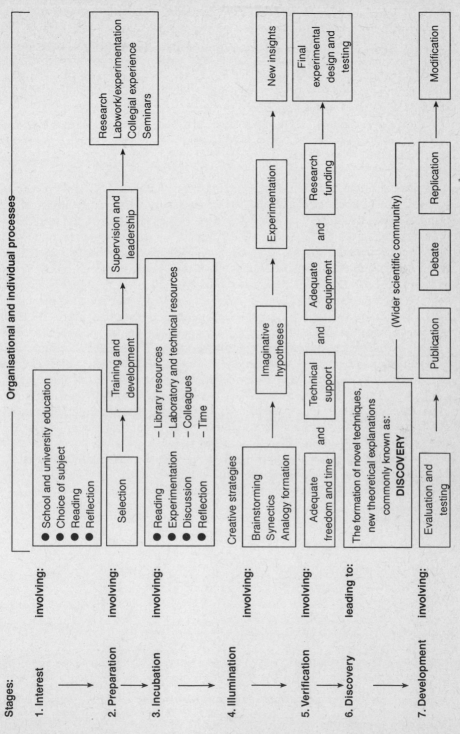

Figure 2 An elaboration of Wallas' processes of scientific discovery

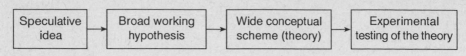

Figure 3   The process of discovery

(d) the integration of the hypothesis into a larger scientific framework,
(e) the precipitation of reasoning in accord with epistemological expectations,
(f) the reorganisation of our understanding of the matter in hand (from Brannigan, 1981).

This explanation is readily recognised as a generalisation of the process of science, and is very different from the logical positivist approach, which as we have seen does not include discovery. It would be most useful to test this theory empirically.

Simonton (1990) proposes a historiometric explanation in which general hypotheses about human behaviour are tested by analysing data in relation to historical individuals. In the case of scientists, Simonton attempts to explain their successes, including discovery, from an analysis of their behaviour within their time. Simonton goes on to provide a general theory of the acquisition of new knowledge. This is once again not an equivalent to discovery, but clearly comes very close to it. Simonton calls his theory 'the chance-configuration theory' and bases it on Campbell's (1960) ideas of blind variation and selective retention. In this theory there are three processes (Simonton, 1988a, 1988b)

(a) the acquisition of new knowledge, the solution of novel problems, requires some means of producing variation (otherwise only older ideas will prevail);
(b) these heterogeneous variations are subjected to consistent variation to winnow out all but those that exhibit adaptive fit;
(c) the variations that have been selected must be preserved and reproduced by some mechanism.

This is clearly based on a biological model such as genetic variation. In scientific ideas this last phase might be the development of a sound theory base to support and retain the new ideas. This theory provides a most interesting cognitive basis of the positive role of chance in discovery, in which chance plays the role of the provider of the necessary 'blind variation'. It should also be tested empirically against discovery.

There are two rather contrasting views of the process of discovery. The first, and perhaps the most commonly held view, is that discovery occurs in an instant. A scientist's mind puts together hitherto unconnected insights and arrives at a reformulation of an existing theory or a completely new one. The other view is an incremental one. It would argue that scientists narrow down errors, improve techniques and gradually bring science to a more accurate state. This increasingly accurate body of science creates anomalies and contradictions from time to time, which call for resolution by way of reformulation. These two views are not necessarily mutually exclusive, but the contrast between them illustrates the difficulty in arriving at an agreed definition of discovery.

Through dedicated enquiry and experimentation, new sets of knowledge may emerge. Progress may be slow and even tortuous at times, but scientific rigour and intellectual honesty set the standards for such research. Francis Bacon (1605) wisely observed: 'If a man will begin with certainties he shall end with doubts; but if he shall be content with doubts, he shall end in certainties.'

Chapter 2

Method, Organisation and Philosophy in Discovery

1 DIFFERING PHILOSOPHICAL VIEWS OF DISCOVERY

The particular scientific method used takes place within a larger conceptual, attitudinal and societal framework. That framework can be seen as beginning in the philosophical system which allows us to see scientific activity in a particular intellectual setting. It also takes place against the backdrop of the economic and social development and prosperity of the state in which it is conducted and, in particular, in the context of that state's science policy. Another influential factor would be the particular organisational framework of the university or commercial laboratory within which the research takes place. For example, one can imagine how different it must be working in a university or other laboratory which emphasises teaching over research, and which allocates small funding for any research that does take place, as opposed to working in an institution where research is an integral and highly valued part of the system. Finally, within these systems at the focal point of a given research project, one must consider the calibre of the principal investigator as a scientist, and as an organiser and leader.

The philosophical backdrop against which science research takes place is an influential force in determining its nature and the experimental methods used. The work of Francis Bacon had a profound effect on the development of our approach to science today. For example, in *The Great Instauration* (1620), he speaks of the major re-organisation needed in science.

2 DISCOVERY AS THE APPLICATION OF LOGIC AND METHOD

Bacon's contribution to the development of experimental science was considerable. He moved science on from an exclusive reliance on the mind's working to a reliance on the facts of nature, which he argued we must learn to allow to speak for themselves. He regarded the mind as being under the influence of many distorting influences:

> For the mind of man is far from the nature of a clear and equal glass wherein the beams of things should reflect according to their true incidence; nay it is rather like an enchanted glass, full of superstition and imposture, if it be not delivered and reduced (Bacon, 1603).

Bacon also had a very strong influence on the Enlightenment of the eighteenth and nineteenth centuries. He considered that scientific progress and discovery should be divided into three clear stages: natural history was the stage of accumulating experiments and observations; 'physics' was the investigation of the lower axioms; and metaphysics was the discovery of nature's 'eternal and fundamental laws'. Significantly, Bacon saw the imagination as the greatest attribute for devising the programme of experimentation and observation, so that the scientist did not waste time 'groping in the dark'. This would appear to correspond to the modern idea of hypothesis generation and experimental design.

Since about the beginning of the twentieth century, discovery in science has been presented as a calm, logical, rational process, in which highly intelligent and very focused individuals reach important insights in an entirely planned way. This *post hoc* type of rational presentation can be very misleading, not only to the general public, but perhaps also to some scientists. It ignores a number of important factors in the discovery process, which if they were not ignored could be incorporated as useful processes into a scientist's work. This regulated, almost mechanical, picture of discovery is the view espoused by the logical-positivist school, which started as the Vienna Group.

The logical-positivist approach to scientific discovery describes well the process of testing theories and provides a logic for that. However, it does not describe the process of developing theories, proposing new formulations or developing new insights. It describes the process referred to by Kuhn (1962) as 'normal science'. 'Revolutionary' science and discovery are excluded from its framework, probably because neither could be described as logical. In fact, discovery presents a challenge to the existing logic and is outside it. It seems as though one part of Bacon's insight has been emphasised and another part (the part dealing with the generation of ideas) has been ignored.

Logical positivism, or logical empiricism, has tended to formulate the problems of science in terms of mathematical logic. The form of, and logical relations between assertions, rather than the content of such assertions, is used to judge scientific theories within this philosophy of science. According to this point of view:

> Scientific theories were conceived of as being...axiomatic (or axiomatizable) systems whose connection with experience was to be achieved by 'rules of

interpretation', the general characteristics of which could again be stated in formal terms (Shapere, 1992).

Thus, this school of thought has dealt with the justification of scientific theories in terms of the (inductive or deductive) logical connections between the theories and experimental observations. In an attempt to demonstrate the logical division between science and pseudoscience, Karl Popper (1963) set out rules for the 'game' of science as follows. Firstly, a hypothesis is proposed which makes bold predictions, both unexpected in the light of previous knowledge and falsifiable by means of existing experimental techniques. (Popper firmly rejected the inductivist view that factual propositions can be derived from facts.) Next, repeated experiments are performed in an attempt to falsify the predictions of the hypothesis in a way agreed upon by the scientific community. If the results of the experiment are agreed to falsify the hypothesis, it is rejected; otherwise, it is labelled 'corroborated' and further attempts to falsify it are invited.

A key feature of this model is Popper's insistence on a falsifiable theory. In other words, it must be conceivable that observations could be made which would refute the theory. Thus, scientists who are testing a theory must seek those results which, if observed, would prove that theory false. Those who search for confirmations are, in Popper's (1963) view, misdirecting their energies:

> Confirmations should count only if they are the result of risky predictions ... if, unenlightened by the theory in question, we should have expected an event which was incompatible with the theory — an event which would have refuted the theory.

In other words, only failed attempts at falsification can be regarded as 'confirming' evidence. In fact, what is generally regarded as a confirmation of a risky prediction is simply a falsification of another opposite theory.

Critics of Popper are quick to point out that most scientists do not really seek to falsify theories, but rather to confirm them. Indeed, Popper (1959) himself voiced this concern (Popper, 1959, p. 42):

> For it is always possible to find some way of evading falsification, for example by introducing *ad hoc* an auxiliary hypothesis, or by changing *ad hoc* a definition. It is even possible without logical inconsistency to adopt the position of simply refusing to acknowledge any falsifying experience whatsoever.

According to Popper, this reduces the scientific status of such theories. It is worth noting that Philip Kitcher's (1993) account of the scientific community is quite different:

> ... once a field has established a set of paradigm answers to application questions, further instantiations of its schemata are no longer on a par. Many questions to which an available schema could be directed are not regarded as significant because the record of success in instantiating the schema gives everyone confidence

that they could (with time and effort) be answered, and the task of grinding out the details looks like hack work ... the questions that now appear significant are those that seem to involve special difficulties of producing instantiations. These questions raise the hope that when they are answered the community will obtain corrected, completed, or extended schemata.

In other words, the interesting problems to scientists are the falsifications, just as Popper would wish.

While Popper recommended advancing 'bold' hypotheses, the methods employed for generating such hypotheses were deemed irrelevant to the justification or falsification game. The philosophy he advanced in *The Logic of Scientific Discovery* (1958) placed discovery well outside the realm of the logical scheme he defined (Kantorovich, 1993).

Imre Lakatos (1978) modified Popper's falsificationism to present what he felt was a picture of the scientific method more consistent with the history of science. Recognising that most successful hypotheses are 'born refuted', he proposed scientific research programs consisting of 'hard cores' of central hypotheses and 'protective belts' of auxiliary hypotheses. These programs are not to be discarded after a single refutation and are regarded as successful or progressive if they maintain a positive balance of corroborated novel predictions relative to unexplained anomalies, compared with competing research programs. Like his predecessors, Lakatos presented 'logics of discovery' which gave rules for accepting or rejecting hypotheses, theories or research programs; no rules were given for generating them.

Paul Feyerabend (1970) comes closer to giving a prescription for generating scientific theories. He writes:

... there is not a single rule, however plausible, and however firmly grounded in epistemology, that is not violated at some time or other. It becomes evident that such violations are not accidental events, they are not results of insufficient knowledge or of inattention which might have been avoided. On the contrary, we see that they are necessary for progress. Indeed, one of the most striking features of recent discussions in the history and philosophy of science is the realization that events and developments, such as the invention of atomism in antiquity, the Copernican Revolution, the rise of modern atomism, ... the gradual emergence of the wave theory of light, occurred only because some thinkers either decided not to be bound by certain 'obvious' methodological rules, or because they unwittingly broke them.

In focusing on essential elements for scientific growth and progress, Feyerabend singles out discovery and proposes an anti-method 'anything goes' approach which has left more than a few scientists uncomfortable. However, Root-Bernstein (1988) points out:

Why not admit that discoveries derive from the ways in which particular scientists logically go about their work? Then, given that different scientists practice different styles of research, and that not all of them make discoveries, it should be possible to identify the styles that most often pay off. Surely, any mental activity that contributes directly to scientific discoveries should be recognised as scientific method. If such activities are not acknowledged by the prevailing view of how scientists use logic and reason, that does not mean the activities are illogical. It means that the prevailing view is too narrow to account for how scientists really think. The task, then, is to redefine the scientific method in a way that accounts for the process of discovery.

3 DISCOVERY AS PROBLEM-SOLVING

Problem-solving is, of course, directly related to science research. However, can discovery itself be regarded as an example of problem-solving? Clearly, the discovery process does involve extensive problem-solving, but is it entirely problem-solving? If this is the case, with the proper heuristics, machines could be programmed to do this for us. This is the basis of Simon's (1985) argument. He has devised a computer program to act in a problem-solving way and has shown that, given the proper heuristic and all the necessary information, it has been able to derive Kepler's third law from information available to Galileo. However, Csikszentmihalyi (1988) identifies a major problem with this theory, in the way in which the problem is formulated or defined. With our present understanding, we can now see how Kepler's law could be derived in this way, but it is not clear who or what would formulate the question in the way Kepler did. According to Bauer (1992), in a book critical of the adherence to the scientific method:

> One of the things wrong with the popular, classical definition of the scientific method is the implication that solitary people can successfully do good science, for example frame hypotheses and test them. In practice, however, the people who put forward the hypotheses are not usually the same people who apply the best tests to them.

The formulation of the problem in a particular way has long been seen as a major component of discovery. For example, Dewey (1917) and Wertheimer (1945) have drawn attention to the importance of formulating the question in the right way. Newton's formulation of gravity as a force and Darwin's of the process of natural selection are as much examples of posing the problem in the 'right' way as they are examples of problem-solving. In fact, much of the related problem-solving came later, much later. As Einstein and Infeld (1938) put it:

> The formulation of a problem is often more essential than its solution, which may be merely a matter of mathematical or experimental skill. To raise new questions, new possibilities, to regard old problems from a new angle, requires creative imagination and marks real advance in science.

Problem-solving ability would appear to be an important component of creativity or discovery, and, as such, ability in problem solving is important in scientists oriented to discovery. Problem-finding may be an even more important ability.

Perkins (1992) suggests a model for the process of discovery which integrates several cognitive approaches to problems. In fact, the model seems to characterise the process of scientific discovery in a way similar to that described by the Nobel laureates in this study. These scientists were mostly uncomfortable with my description of their work as creative. They seemed to see part of it as creative, other parts as collaborative, other parts simply routine. They described their work as mostly hard work, aided by the emergence of useful insights from time to time.

A model which Perkins refers to as 'smart foraging' fits their descriptions of the process of scientific discovery better. His model takes issue with the conventional view of creative thinking and invention as 'heroic quest'. This 'heroic quest' vision of invention is part and parcel of a tendency to elevate inventors to epic hero status, which includes the following ingredients:

(a) Heroic persistence. The inventor persists for a considerable time with little progress.
(b) Unexpected encounter. The inventor eventually encounters a subtle clue from an unexpected direction.
(c) The gift of insight. 'The inventor has the insight to seize on the clue and make something of it to complete the quest' (Perkins, 1992, p. 239).

This vision is probably the most commonly held vision of discovery, and lays almost total emphasis on a gifted individual. As Perkins points out, this model is a bit too plausible and neat to be entirely believable, and is not helpful in leading us to understand the process of discovery. For example, by its emphasis on individual characteristics, it does not empower us to develop programmes to make discovery more frequent. Perkins' 'smart foraging' model, on the other hand, assumes a familiarity with the area of science on the part of the scientist who is 'well tuned to the topography of ideas' (Perkins, 1992). His ideas build on Newell and Simon's (1972) model, which introduced the notion of the 'problem space'. This 'problem space' is the area of the world of knowledge with which the scientist is familiar, and contains problems that are obvious to him or her. The scientist aims to arrive at a new target state which will provide an advance on the existing state of knowledge or an insight in the defined problem space.

Perkins divides the problem space between 'Klondike spaces', where you are looking everywhere for clues to the solution of your problem, and 'homing spaces', which help you to home in on the solution. Instead of the 'heroic quest', Perkins suggests 'smart foraging' along the following lines (adapted from Perkins, 1992, p. 244):

(a) Klondike space. The search is conducted in an open space, seeking clues from whatever source.

(b) Well-adapted search. The search is adapted to the character of the particular Klondike space in terms of size and other characteristics of an appropriate kind.

(c) Probable encounter. The well-adapted search makes contact with a relevant probable clue, presuming that a solution exists.

(d) The prepared mind's detection of promise. The clue is detected by a mind well prepared for the clue, by immersion in the problem and in the literature.

(e) Discrimination of potential. Here the discoverer-scientist must be able to distinguish valuable clues from diversions.

(f) Effective pursuit. Discovery involves following through in the 'homing space' on good clues.

This presents a very different picture of discovery from our traditional 'heroic quest' view. It is a more gradual process, and one more dependent on other colleagues and on the wider support of the laboratory and the general organisation, than the rather lonely picture of discovery painted in the past.

Based on problem-solving theories, but also on artificial intelligence, new views of discovery are emerging which have become possible to conceive because of the extensive possibilities of computers to provide virtually unlimited processing power. Some texts, including Shrager and Langley (1990), support the Simon (1985) idea (that machines can make discoveries) by suggesting a computational model to aid — or perhaps even supplant — the processes involved in scientific discovery. This is indeed a logical extension of Simon's work, and is an interesting new interpretation of the discovery process. If this were to lead to the development of advanced expert systems within an artificial intelligence framework, this could be very promising and exciting.

The development of the 'supercomputer' certainly opens up the possibility that computational programmes can be developed which will be able to approach the solution of problems, and even the suggestion of hypotheses, based on the availability of computer-observed patterns and analogies in several fields. In theory at least, the processes that appear to characterise human scientific discovery could be replicated in supercomputers, equipped with humanoid strategies of computation.

In practice this is rather far from reality, and may even be a reduction of discovery to computation, when scientific insight development may well be something peculiar to the human mind. This is an area with the prospect of many exciting developments.

4   DISCOVERY AS THE DEVELOPMENT OF INSIGHT

In a philosophical challenge to the logical-positivist view of science, Kantorovich (1993) describes scientific discovery as a kind of natural selection, in which the successful paradigms survive scrutiny. He also sees discovery as a natural continuous process, quite separate from 'justification', a term he uses for the *post hoc* rational testing of a theoretical position. He regards discovery, not as the province of the unique genius but as open to all scientists, provided they do not kill off their capacity to discover with the exclusive use of logical thinking.

Recently, Kantorovich (1993) has undertaken to include the process of discovery in his account of the philosophy of science. He presents an evolutionary epistemology to explain the rational development of science and the development of both inborn cognitive machinery and human knowledge as a whole. An analogy is drawn to biological evolution, in which a number of blind mutations of genetic material are exposed to selection forces to determine which genotypes will survive into the next generation.

Within science, the blind mutations or recombinations are serendipitous events or discoveries: either eureka events or persistent anomalies leading to new research aims. Since scientific problems are underdetermined, and their solutions cannot be uniquely determined there is necessarily an element of blindness when a solution is proposed.

Some would argue that the scientific world view limits the possible solutions proposed for any given problem. Kantorovich agrees, and further includes our cognitive apparatus as a limiting factor on a range of variation of theories. However, he claims that both our organic make-up and our scientific tradition are themselves the results of evolution due to biological and cultural selective processes. It is further argued that at least some of the new information generated by scientists is generated in a decidedly non-blind manner, by means of deductive inference or mathematical derivation. This would seem to comprise the course of 'normal' science within an established paradigm.

Kantorovich (1993) argues, however, that what starts as 'normal' science may turn into a revolutionary departure:

> One of the major ways of transcending an established state of knowledge is to do it unintentionally while trying to solve some problem within the confines of the prevailing paradigm.

Serendipity may manifest itself not only in what is found experimentally but also in the ideas or associations that suggest themselves in the interpretation of data or hypotheses. According to Kantorovich (1993), in order to cultivate serendipity and thus maximise the number of 'blind variations' (hypotheses) at play in the evolution of science, one ought to:

> ... be engaged in solving more than one problem at a time, to be engaged with problems which do not seem to be related to each other, and to be aware of as many problems as possible. And in general, one should not restrict his domain of interest to his current narrow area of research.

Such an approach not only allows opportunities for the chance association due to one's intrapsychic process of creation but it may also spark creativity through interpsychic processes within a research team or the scientific community as a whole.

Once 'mutations' in scientific thought have been introduced, selection pressures are brought to bear, first by the scientist who originates the new idea (in deciding whether it is worthy of mention) and next by the scientific community. Selections may be made due to experimental reproducibility, coherence of a theory, simplicity of a theory and so on. Depending on the environment of science, selection criteria may vary. A theory well adapted to the current environment might perish with the advent of a new environment. Following selection, successful 'mutations' are propagated in the scientific literature and in the training of new scientists. The 'migration' of scientists from one field to another may increase the propagation of successfully adapted theories, as well as increasing the pool of material for 'recombination' in the next round of hypothesis development.

5 DISCOVERY AS ANALOGY-BASED, 'BISOCIATION' OR METAPHORIC

Analogical reasoning

Analogy is defined in the *Oxford English Dictionary* (1989) as:

Equivalence or likeness in relations; resemblance of things with regard to some circumstance or effects.

Metaphor is defined as:

The figure of speech in which a name or descriptive term is transformed to some object different from, but analogous to, that to which it is properly applicable.

Many scientists believe analogies play an important part in discovery. Johnson-Laird (1988) concludes that:

A scientific problem can be illuminated by the discovery of a profound analogy, and a mundane problem can be solved in a similar way.

He goes on to describe the use of analogies within the problem space as:

...linking two regions within the space. The more remote they are from one another, the longer the chain of links, and granted that in its construction there are always different possible continuations leading to different domains, the harder will it be to construct (Johnson-Laird, p. 267).

This seems very close to Koestler's view of scientific creativity, and it may be that no significant difference exists between these two terms (Koestler, 1976).

Hesse (1963) relates analogical thinking to model-building, and regards them both as essential to the development of scientific theory. In the present study, Ernst states:

> I always use analogies for explanations of facts. You need a comprehensive knowledge of existing facts to get ideas and to understand. They really help me.

Elion is of the view that analogies are very important:

> Analogies have been helpful to me even on a chemical level. For example, if you read about something where, because we were particularly working in an area where you would try to mimic the natural product, but just make it a little bit off so that the organism couldn't use it; in other words, you would make a false polypeptide or peptide that might get into the nucleic acid and foul things up for the organism. Well you read about other people looking at different amino acids and proteins and they made certain changes that really had this effect, try that one, maybe putting a sulphur in place of an oxygen would work in this area as well, so there are a lot of analogies in science where if you keep reading and you listen, then you can see how that applies to what you are doing.

She tells us the role of analogy in developing her new ideas:

> New ideas don't come completely out of the blue. You have to have the idea from somewhere. Maybe the analogy is a little far fetched sometimes, but I think analogy is absolutely necessary in a field like ours. It was particularly true when vitamins were discovered. People began to think of vitamins . . . to prevent bacteria from growing, to prevent cells from growing, because the cells needed this nutrient to grow, and obviously if you mess it up it couldn't grow, so those were analogies. Folic acid is an antagonist, folic acid is a vitamin, that was one of the first antileukaemic drugs, was an antifolic acid. So the analogies were certainly there.

Bacon (1620) rejected the early magical ways of thinking—which included the use of false analogies based on observed and often superficial similarities. Similarities of colour or of form were often, in those days, held to hold some meaning as to function. An example of this is superficial resemblance between the root Satyrion and the testicles. Though he regarded analogies as highly useful in providing heuristics for discovery, he saw that:

> . . . the mind of man is far from the nature of a clear and equal glass, (mirror) . . . but rather is like an enchanted glass, full of superstition and imposture, if it not be delivered and reduced.

Yet he saw the use of analogy as the imagination of man at work on the natural world, and thus a primary source of ideas in relation to scientific experiment, if properly disciplined and controlled. According to Park (1984), Bacon regarded analogical reasoning as 'basic not only to the workings of the human mind, but also to the structure of the world'.

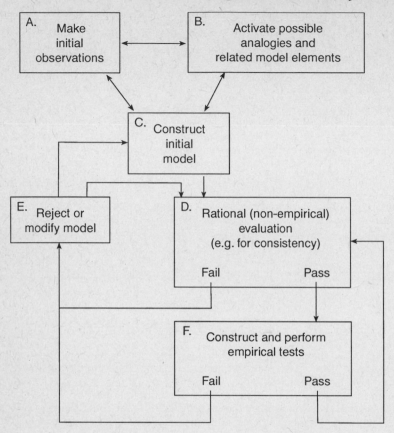

Figure 4   The Clement (1988) model of the scientific process

Clement (1988) places the use of analogies in the development phase of discovery in science as shown in Figure 4. In his description of hypothesis formation (a much neglected field), Clement brings together the ideas of hypothetico-deduction plus induction, creative intuition and analogies and successive refinements of explanatory hypotheses. His model of scientific discovery puts analogical reasoning into the experimental frame of science. Analogy and metaphor seem to be very close to Koestler's 'bisociation'. All three link thinking in one plane with thinking in another.

Bisociation

Koestler (1976) put forward the idea that discovery is characterised by the linking of ideas from two separate and often unrelated areas to one another.

He gives a graphic example of this in Kekule's discovery of the structure of benzine rings. Kekule was half asleep and dreamt of snakes chasing their tails. When he woke up his dream seemed to relate to his work on the structure of benzine. He postulated that benzine was a structure in a ring form, and later showed this to be true. Koestler (1976, p. 135) described 'bisociation' as follows:

> I have coined the term 'bisociation' in order to make a distinction between the routine skills of thinking on a 'plane' as it were, and the creative act which, as I shall try to show, always operates on more than one plane.

Bisociation, according to Koestler, was to 'connect previously unconnected matrices of experience'.

In a recent study, Root-Bernstein (1994) showed that:

> Interviews revealed that the strategies of switching fields and exploring multiple lines of research concomitantly were conscious ones among the long-term, high-impact scientists, and that the strategies were adopted in the belief that once a scientist has made a major contribution to a field he or she has seen everything of importance to be seen, and that the only way to get a fresh view of a subject is to enter a new field in which one is a relative novice.

Dasgupta (1992) sees the metaphor as a powerful creative tool, enabling the scientist to experience mentally, some fact or process which can not be seen. Further, according to Dasgupta, it is a useful heuristic, which helps the scientist learn from parallels from other areas. He cites Lavoisier's metaphor of breathing as like a candle burning, as helpful in leading him to suggest the correct chemistry of respiration.

Scientific method

Though our philosophy of science influences our thinking with regard to the way we practise science, it does not lead directly to a scientific method. The classical scientific method contains the following elements:

(a) hypothesis development,
(b) data gathering,
(c) development or refinement of the hypothesis,
(d) further data gathering or testing,
(e) development of a theory.

In reality, however, few experiments proceed on these lines. Sinderman (1985) points to a more evolutionary process in the development of scientific insight. He describes an iterative process, rather than a scheduled one. He points to the need to know more about these evolutionary processes, rather than the need for models or schedules of experimentation. In particular, Sinderman highlights the need to know more about the origin of research ideas. It is really only after the initial research ideas have been gained that the appropriate scientific method is sought. Sinderman (1985, p. 22) is conscious, too, of the wider role of the principal investigator:

> Superficially, it would seem enough to plan the research, delegate responsibilities for its execution, and analyze the results. Successful scientists recognise early, however, that this is merely the framework for a complex and continuing relationship with people, who bring all their own priorities, moods and idiosyncrasies, to the laboratory each morning, along with their competencies.

Can we 'plan' discoveries? Certainly many scientists, including Fleming, are of the view that you cannot. Root-Bernstein (1994) tells us:

> It is not surprising to discover that when Fleming toured a British pharmaceutical company that was mass-producing penicillin during WW II — with its regiments of workers, gleaming sterile rooms, and precise production schedules — he remarked that it was all very impressive, but he couldn't have made the discovery there. You need conditions of creative dissonance and limited sloppiness to be able to make breakthroughs. Typical business management consisting of control of resources, directing of employees, budgets, timetables, and a general striving for maximum efficiency, as it is taught at Harvard, Chicago, or Stanford, is inimical to such research.
>   It is also clear that the style of research Fleming undertook would not be permissible in many institutions. Outside of his clinical duties, he had complete freedom to research whatever he felt most important — even the freedom to indulge his bacterial painting. This was a strategy of research for him, a way of courting serendipity.

This brief review suggests to us that logic is a necessary but insufficient basis for discovery. As Poincare puts it: 'It is by logic that we prove, but by intuition that we invent.' Imaginative leaps are needed, and should take place in an evolutionary way, building on the insights of others. Into this evolutionary process, chance factors are known to play an important part. Given that the scientist is prepared well, and is deeply committed to a topic, observations of phenomena and new structuring may occur. These often come as a great surprise, and do not fit into existing theories or paradigms. They are surprising because they are new discoveries. Because they are surprising, they are often seen as having their origins in chance. However, are these random, magical chance occurrences, or the workings of a prepared and devoted mind, reaching out beyond confirmation to the as-yet unborn but powerful new insight which is discovery?

There is a discernible trend in the philosophy of science towards a consideration of discovery as the successful culmination of good research. This is in contrast to the concerns of the logical positivists, who regarded discovery as outside their purview. The second trend that is noticeable is towards a realisation of the group, the collaborative nature of the scientific research process. This latter trend is supportive of the central argument presented in this text.

6 THE ORGANISATIONAL DIMENSION OF DISCOVERY IN SCIENCE

The role of the individual scientist, however elaborately supported technically, or whatever one's philosophical view, remains embedded within some sort of an organisational and social framework. This organisational dimension of discovery in science has been largely ignored by organisation theorists or management thinkers. Some scientists, however, have made substantial contributions in this area, including Beveridge, Conant, Polanyi and Root-Bernstein.

Organisational processes appear to be of considerable, perhaps even decisive, importance in discovery. All Nobel laureates in this study and most others are members of advanced, well-organised laboratories and institutions. It seems likely that those scientists who have made substantial discoveries have done so, at least in part, because they had been favourably located in well-organised laboratories, in highly developed societies. Existing data on the distribution of substantial discovery in science suggests strongly that exceptional scientific talent in science, even coupled with high levels of creativity, are unlikely to be sufficient for scientists to discover. If such people are located in laboratories where inadequate organisational resources are at their disposal, discovery is unlikely to occur. This is not simply the familiar argument that 'more resources will lead to more discovery', rather it is an argument for more resources and a more developed scientific organisation.

Beveridge (1950) was very conscious of the organisational dimension in science, and discussed it under three headings: tactical — the organisation within the laboratory — strategic — the province of the research director — and policy — the level at which planning for research and funding on a general scale is carried out. At the 'tactical' level, which is the main focus of this book, Beveridge suggests the fairly standard stages shown in Table 4 in the process of research. Beveridge is given on the left and the possible organisational dimensions on the right. Beveridge's thinking suggests that substantial, but often taken for granted, organisational support is required for scientific research. This could be the basis of empirical research of a comparative nature.

Root-Bernstein (1989, p. 202) gives the model of discovery shown in Figure 5, which is descriptive of the processes involved in discovery mainly from the point of view of the individual scientist. Some reference is made to cultural and institutional milieu in the outer framing of the model. He says further:

> I have not drawn an explicit input for the cultural context of science. I have just sort of assumed that the process is embedded in a particular context, which includes everything from the economics and politics of science, to educational policies, religion, and social organisation.

Table 4 Beveridge's stages and their organisational implications

Beveridge	Organisational dimensions implied in Beveridge
Critical review of the literature	Library, computer support, training
Thorough collection of field data	Funding, technical support, storage, computer
All information marshalled and correlated	Computer training
Problem is defined and broken into specific questions	Training
Intelligent guesses are made as to explanations	Group discussion
Hypotheses are developed	Creativity development
Experiments are designed to test experiments	Training, leadership, discussion
Experiment is planned, assessed and carried out	Training, leadership

This model, however, implies significant organisational support. It implies 'Harvard' rather than St Everyone's College, with its emphasis on mass teaching and its poor support for excellence in research. Conant (1948), as we have seen in Chapter 1, describes the process of discovery as shown in Figure 6. Conant gives the example of atomic theory to illustrate this process. He described the Greek atomists' ideas of nature being composed of ultimate particles as a speculative idea. It took a very long time for Dalton in 1800 to come up with a broad working hypothesis in relation to the atomic composition of simple elements and compounds. This only happened later, after he had shown how fruitful his conceptual scheme was in chemical experiments.

If we examine the processes of research described by Beveridge, Root-Bernstein and Conant, we see that there is an important role for the group and the organisation, as well as for the individual. The process of research is gradual, slow, painstaking, and usually takes place within a laboratory. Kantorovich (1993) points to the gradual, often painstakingly slow process which is research:

> Personally, a scientist may make very few scientific discoveries, if any during his lifetime; most scientific discoveries are products of collective efforts. Therefore, it is sometimes difficult to judge who participated in, or contributed to, the discovery; sometimes it is perhaps a whole community which should be credited. If the process extends over a long period of time, only the final step in the process is regarded as a discovery. Yet the contributions of the other participants are sometimes no less important than the contribution which constituted the breakthrough.

In saying this, he recognises the wider role of the principal scientist as a leader, supervisor, mentor and friend. What all this means is that we are in the middle of a major change in our approach to discovery, and in particular in the

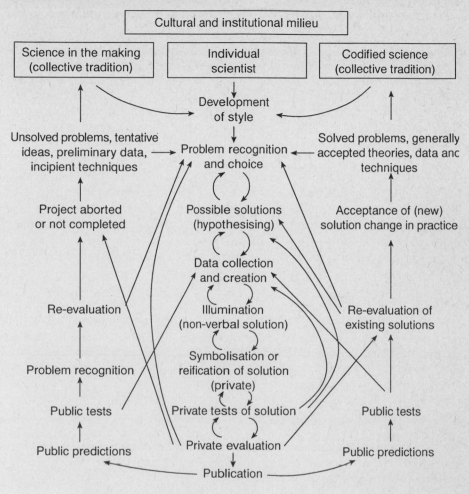

Figure 5 Root-Bernstein's model of the discovery process

role that an organisation or creativity plays in discovery. It is possible that the role of the organisation of the research laboratory is greater in relation to discovery than is the role of creativity.

Clearly this description of the process of discovery is very different from the traditional 'instant illumination' that pervades the literature. It suggests, too, a

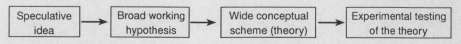

Figure 6 The generation of ideas in brainstorming

considerable role for the group, and for the organisation in which the group is embedded.

In recounting the story of scientific discovery, it is not surprising that scientists speak only of puzzling through a confusing and often misleading theoretical jungle. They rarely make any reference to the organisational environment in which the discovery takes place, or of the extensive range of human resources that were at their disposal. Scientists are conscious of using these resources, and they tend to use them well and value the help they get, but when describing their discovery processes they simply do not think it relevant to bring in another dimension, such as the organisational one. In a similar way they do not usually mention the sums of money that were devoted to the project, though they are well aware that without money, organisation and human resources, they would not have made their discoveries. Even the largest projects requiring thousands of scientists are not described in organisational terms, but in terms of solving a problem or testing a theory. This may surprise organisational thinkers, but it is probably a very natural and sensible focus on the core of their concerns, which are scientific ones.

Because these descriptions of science in practice so often emphasise the thinking process of the individual scientist who has made the particular discovery, there is a tendency to concentrate on the characteristics of these talented individuals. There is an abundance of literature which studies the scientist, the genius, the creative individual, and draws generalisations from these studies. However, one of the weaknesses in drawing conclusions from studies of the nature of individual creative people is that they themselves are often not the 'onlie begetters' of new science, but rather those individuals who have put together the most recent details of the puzzle. Newton said 'If I have seen further, it is because I stand upon the shoulders of giants', recognising that the process of discovery takes place over a long time and depends for its relative completion on the work of many others, in a variety of differing fields.

Hegel (1971) put it more colourfully:

> ...(the inventor)...is like the man who finds himself among workers who are building a stone arch whose general structure is invisibly present as an idea. He so happens to be the last in line; when he puts his stone into place, the arch supports itself. As he places his stone he sees the whole edifice is an arch, says so and passes for the inventor.

Hegel's metaphor is rather dismissive of the individual role of the inventor, but, nevertheless, there is a sense in which it accurately describes what occurs. Discoverers stand on other's shoulders; Newton stood on the shoulders of Hooke, Huygens, Fermat, Descartes, Kepler and Galileo, among many others. In discovering the structure of the genetic material, Crick and Watson depended on the work of Franklin, Bernal, Bragg, Chargaff, Wilkins, Mendelsohn and Stahl—and this is to mention only the most proximate shoulders. When they came up with their structure for genetic material, they were among the first people for whom that was possible. The invisible arch was almost complete. All the components were available, the techniques were known; Watson and Crick placed the last stone in that particular arch, and shouted: 'The double helix'. The activities of Crick and Watson in developing their insights into the structure of DNA, though interesting in themselves, make it clear, as do most other descriptions of discovery, that the process of arriving at insights was based on a great many other insights and techniques, without which their particular insights would not have been possible.

There is an understandable fascination with the individuals who are credited with great discoveries, but if we observe only the activities of those great scientists, and are not aware of the sometimes very substantial organisational support which they had, then we omit an important, possibly decisive, dimension to discovery. Also, we may observe only a particular point in a process, i.e. when the process of solving a particular scientific problem has reached a new level of clarity. We may not be aware of the organisational processes which brought the scientists to this new level of insight.

The fact is that most of our most distinguished scientists, including all of those in the present study, have carried out their research in well-resourced, well-organised institutions. These institutions have managed to create the right circumstances for creative scientific work to take place, within this organisational framework. This somewhat paradoxical situation of scientific freedom and discretion for the principal investigator and the scientific team, within a controlled and well-resourced organisational environment, appears to be what the discovery-oriented scientist needs. Security and stability over a long term, coupled with the possibility of great freedom to experiment, to explore blind alleys, to follow hunches, to recruit just the right people, is just what is needed. Such an abundant environment can also provide the stimulation of gifted colleagues, the inspiration of enthusiastic leaders, encouragement, patience and a secret garden to explore the aromas of an elusive flower.

The figures of Nobel laureates by country cited by Eigen in Table 1, and those in Tables 2 and 3, might be taken as an argument for a sociological interpretation, and we have seen that sociological effects do exist. However, since discovery occurs only in a very small number of laboratories, within a given sociological environment, an organisational explanation is also needed. It seems more than just a wild guess to suggest that there is something about the organisational situation of scientists who discover that is different from the situation in all other research laboratories, whether they have scientists who are creative or not. It is also possible that not all discoveries will be made by creative scientists; some may be stumbled upon, others may make discoveries by hard work and a deep interest in an area, when less 'creative' scientists do not. Hence an organisational framework related to discovery may be even more useful than a creativity oriented one.

Andrews (1967) studied 'creative ability, the laboratory environment, and scientific performance' and based his findings on the same data as used by Pelz and Andrews (1976). Creative ability was measured using the remote associates test, a test that measures people's ability to think of remote and unusual associations. Performance was assessed by colleagues on the basis of the scientific or technical contribution. Interestingly, no relationship was found between creative ability as tested and creative output as assessed. Andrews explanation 'Our best explanation is that creative ability can hurt as well as help (a person's performance) depending on the situation' does not seem adequate. Though it could be that the particular organisation used in that study (a bureaucratic science organisation) was discouraging of real creativity, in that it might rock the bureaucratic boat, Andrews seems to hint at this; he says, for example: '...some R&D labs may not actually want as much creativity as they claim.' Of course, creative output would appear to be closer to discovery than creative potential, and this is one of the very few studies which came close to examining scientific performance.

Other researchers (notably Simonton, 1988b) have attempted to account for differences in levels of discovery in science in a historical way. They hoped to achieve this by allocating responsibility to the psychological characteristics of the day, the 'zeitgeist'—the spirit of the times. Whether it be the society in which they are born, state support for science or university support for their projects, scientists usually do not acknowledge the contribution of the organisation to their work. Most frequently, the organisation is actually invisible to the scientists. From the individual scientist's point of view, this invisibility is probably necessary to protect him or her from becoming too involved in areas outside science, such as administration. In other words, the invisible nature of that which has supported them frees them to be creative. If it were otherwise, it could side-track them and be harmful to their creative energy.

From the viewpoint of those concerned with the organisation of science and in particular the facilitation of creative science, this organisation cannot be invisible. It must be studied, examined, experimented with. Otherwise, the organisational determinants of discovery cannot be established and the possibility would not exist to replicate discovery-favourable conditions where they do not exist at present.

7   THE ABSENCE OF AN EXPLICIT ORGANISATIONAL THEORY OF DISCOVERY IN SCIENCE

Organisation theory is now a well-developed field of study, and some of its subdivisions might well be open to application in the area of science research. Areas such as decision-making, motivation, leadership, selection and training and development might all be the subject of experimentation in science projects, with a view to evaluating their effectiveness. Yet very little literature can be found citing studies of this kind, in relation to the organisation of science research in laboratories. (Studies do exist of the organisation of science at policy level.)

Within organisation theory, many areas are comparative, such as the comparisons of organisation type (e.g. mechanistic compared to organic organisations). Other areas are concerned with the interaction of organisational systems and with the measurement of effectiveness and productivity. Most discovery in science takes place in small university laboratories, not in large industrial ones. There seems to a certain irony here, since by definition large commercial laboratories are 'better' organised than the rather 'loose' and (some would say) 'amateurish' organisation of the university. However, university research has a number of significant advantages, which also illustrate the inappropriate nature of much organisational theory to research work.

Firstly, they are free. Freedom is always a relative concept; no one is totally free as there are constraints of ethics, money, equipment and time. Nevertheless, freedom does exist in a very real sense. University researchers are free to think any way they wish and they can explore what may or may not be blind alleys. Only they are responsible for their judgements as to what to pursue and what to ignore. Secondly, they are frequently motivated by genuinely high levels of curiosity, and by the wish to pry into strange and unconventional corners of the world of nature. Thirdly, they have easy access to other disciplines and can hold discussions concerning wider areas, and involving larger groups, than their industrial counterparts.

In spite of these obvious differences, it is surprising how influential the ideas of Adam Smith, Frederick Taylor and Henry Ford have been in the design of organisations. However, in many cases they have been either unsuitable or even harmful. The ideas of the conveyor belt, of extreme task specialisation, and of the hierarchical division of labour have strongly influenced the organisational structure and processes of the modern hospital, the university and even, in some cases, the research laboratory. Much of this is simply the application of rational principles to the organisation of complex work situations. However, it can also lead to an important level of blindness to the basic aims for which such organisations exist, in favour of excessive emphasis on the processes of organising. Organisation is, or should be, a tool to achieve certain goals, not an end in itself.

Nevertheless, when large funds are involved, those providing the money have an understandable need to see responsibility allocated in clear and identifiable ways, and progress apparent in line with objectives. Some research laboratories, especially larger ones, have a tendency to try to organise the research in projects, subdividing the problem area and allocating pieces of the puzzle to projects. The research director co-ordinates the activities of all projects and is responsible for each of the principal investigators. In this way the research yields an outcome which is 'satisfactory' to the organisation. In other words, research becomes predictable. In science, however, discovery is not predictable and does not seem to flourish in such circumstances.

Attempts to confine science research to an industrial model have never really worked. Much of what goes on in commercial laboratories can be regarded as development rather than research. The organisational processes related to development are likely to be quite different from those related to discovery.

Science research is now a very substantial part of the world economy and deserves a better organisational theory base than it has so far attained. Most existing textbooks, models and theories are based on our industrial past, and on examples of organisation taken mainly from traditional models such as the army, the church, the bureaucracy and the manufacturing plant. These organisations all exist in order to ensure that activities are carried out in a standardised way, and seem quite inappropriate, and possibly harmful, to the organisation of exploratory scientific research, the aim of which is to produce novel and unique solutions to scientific problems.

8 SUMMARY

It is likely that philosophy and method have both played significant roles in influencing the nature and process of scientific research. The role of organisation in relation to discovery may well be a rather neglected field of study. The next chapter reviews the effects that organisations may have on chance, freedom and motivation, in relation to scientific research. Chapter 5 gives an overview of the differing levels of organisation as they impinge on scientific research and the extensive role of organisation in science is explored more fully.

Chapter 3

The Importance of the Individual in Science

1 INTRODUCTION

We shall see in Chapter 4, the differing views that exist on the origins of discovery. These include the scientific method as the source of discovery, the role of problem-solving and the related computational approach, insight development, metaphor, analogy and bisociation. Central to all discovery is the motivated, dedicated scientist, pursuing a problem in persistent and ingenious ways. Such scientists are regarded as creative, when they produce novel and important results. By far the most widespread view in the literature is that only creative people make discoveries. The literature in relation to this is summarised here. Though far less research has been carried out in the areas of the actual professional knowledge development of the scientist, or their persistence and curiosity, this is also referred to in this chapter.

Man has an innate tendency to try to be creative. According to Maritain (1954):

> The creative power of the human spirit craved after pure creation — jealous, as it were, of God, who was tactless enough to create before us.
>
> Over time an important difference seems to have occurred between the meaning of the word creation (which in its fundamental sense implies the bringing into being of something that did not exist before) and the words creative or creativity, which describe imaginative, original and ingenious solutions to existing problems. Perhaps to borrow Herbert Simon's idea of 'bounded rationality' we should think of human creativity more in more bounded terms, as perhaps, 'bounded creativity'.

Most of what we know of the role of the individual in discovery derives from history, biography and anecdotal accounts. Lucretius in the first century AD, writing about 'the nature of things', begins his account as follows:

> For I begin to write of lofty themes; of gods, of the motions of the sky, of the rise
> of things, how all things nature forms, and how they grow, and to perfection rise,
> and into what, by the same nature's laws, those things resolve and die; which as I
> write I call by various names; sometimes 'tis matter, or the first principles or seeds
> of things, or first of bodies, whence all else proceed.

His is an early attempt to bring together all our knowledge of the world around
us into one unified corpus of knowledge; this we later called science.

In Chapter 4 we will see descriptions of the eminent scientists in this study
and also the extensive projects that they managed to obtain (i.e. organise)
agreement to pursue. Many biographies of eminent scientists show their
personality as something quite unusual. They are people of an habitually
distinct view of the world. Scientific revolutions do not commence with
requesting permission to think this way or that; approaches to ideas by creative
scientists are unique and distinct and decidedly independent. Though usually
courteous and self-effacing, eminent scientists are usually so convinced they are
right that they require no affirmation from others. Their characters are
independent and strong minded: to persuade others to devote even modest
funds, time and equipment to some scientific enterprise of doubtful outcome
requires character. Yet they must not be so strong minded as to exclude new
ideas. Here is an intriguing balance — between forcefulness and open-
mindedness — which must be maintained. Einstein said at one stage:

> Most people think it is the intellect which makes a great scientist. They are wrong:
> it is character. (Mackay, 1991).

Attempts to bring discovery under more scientific scrutiny cover a number of
areas of study. They have concentrated in the main on the idea that the
discoverer-scientist is a person whose personal circumstances of social
background or birth order or genetic endowment are highly favourable, or
who has high levels of creativity.

2   CREATIVITY AND DISCOVERY

It might seem intuitively reasonable to expect that discoveries would be made
by scientists with measurable high levels of creativity. However, this has proved
elusive. Attempts to explore the nature and measurement of creativity began in
the 1950s. They can be traced back to the address by Guilford to the American
Psychological Association in 1950 (Guilford 1950). In a later article, Guilford
attributes this growth in research in creativity to the stimulus of the Second
World War, which he says had:

> ...called forth great efforts towards innovation in research and, development,
> culminating in the atomic bomb. The coming of peace that was no peace left us in
> the Cold War, which called for ever accelerating efforts in a contest of intellects.

Inventors' brains were at a premium and there were never enough. We were on the eve of the space age, and rockets were already taking trial flights, stirring our imagination of things to come. The stage was well set then for the psychologist to play his proper role in trying to fathom the creative person and his creative processes (Guilford, 1967a).

Guilford concluded that the evidence from this research indicated that the abilities most related to creative thinking are:

1. Divergent-Production. This pertains to the generation of ideas such as in solving a problem where variety is important, and which is characterised by fluency and flexibility, and the ability to create elaborations.
2. 'Transformation abilities': which relate to revising what one experiences or knows, thereby producing new forms and patterns (Guilford, 1967a).

Both of these forms of creativity would seem to be of considerable value in scientific research, which needs people who can develop divergent and novel problem definitions and work towards their solutions. Although Guilford hypothesised that creative individuals possessed the capacity for divergent thinking to a greater extent than others, subsequent studies attempting to relate these two concepts together have not supported this. Hocevar (1980) found in one study 'that tests of divergent thinking are no better at predicting creativity than its additional and simpler measure of verbal intelligence'. In a six year study on creativity carried out at the University of Berkeley California, the conclusions of Guilford *et al.* (1956) were as follows:

What most generally characterises the creative individual...is his high level of effective intelligence, his openness to experience, his freedom from crippling restraints and impoverishing inhibitions, his aesthetic sensitivity, his culminate flexibility, his independence in thought and action, his high level of creative energy, his unquestioning commitment to creative endeavour, and his unceasing striving for solutions to the ever more difficult problems that he constantly sets for himself.

Fundamentally, the assessment of levels of creativity in science will always depend on informed peer evaluations of individuals or, perhaps more objectively, their products. Mansfield and Busse (1981, p. 5) make an important distinction between evaluating an individual scientist and his or her products, inventions, reformulations, discoveries, patents, etc. They set down criteria for creative scientific products as follows:

First the product must be novel or unusual in relation to other products. ...A creative product must possess some value or appropriateness in addition to novelty.

According to Glover, Ronning and Reynolds (1989), creativity consists of at least four components: (a) the creative process, (b) the creative product, (c) the creative person and (d) the creative situation. Here, the creative product appears to be part of creativity, or presumably equal to discovery. Other definitions of creativity are less ambitious. Vernon (1967, p. 94) has defined creativity in the following way:

> Creativity means a person's capacity to produce new or original ideas, insights, restructurings, inventions, or artistic objects, which are accepted by experts as being of scientific, aesthetic, social, or technological value.

In other words, the creative ideas may be considered to be valuable, but they may not have resulted in any discovery. Their connection with discovery has not been established. Hayes (1989) makes a similar point when he says:

> 'Creative' is a word with many uses. Sometimes it is used to describe the potential of persons to produce creative works whether or not they have produced any work as yet.

Hayes also discusses creativity mainly in terms of its outputs, illustrating a growing dissatisfaction with the 'creativity as such' school of thought. Albert (1983, p. 61) describes the person of genius as

> ...anyone who regardless of other characteristics he may possess or have attributed to him, produces, over a long period of time, a large body of work that has significant influence on many persons for many years....

The origins of this growing dissatisfaction appear to lie in two aspects of the creativity studies, particularly as they may relate to science. The first is the absence of any correlation between creativity as measured on tests and discovery in science. This is important but depends on a number of other factors, not least of which is the need for an agreed definition of scientific discovery. The second is more fundamental. It is easy to form the view on reading the creativity studies that measured creativity *is taken to stand for some outcome* such as discovery. However, we know that creativity is an individual potential which may require other important personality characteristics for it to be expressed in outcome terms.

The next section analyses in some more depth the deficiencies in the creativity studies from the point of view of discovery in science.

3 DEFICIENCIES IN THE CREATIVITY LITERATURE FROM THE PERSPECTIVE OF SCIENTIFIC DISCOVERY

The absence of a link between creativity and discovery

The available literature which examines creativity in the scientific context has two important weaknesses. Attempts to consider organisational factors that are part of everyday science have been few. Secondly, there have been no studies linking creativity with scientific discovery. More precisely, such research of this nature has so far used inadequate measures, particularly of discovery. The first problem is dealt with in Chapter 6. Concerning the latter argument, Boxenbaum's (1991) discussion of 'scientific creativity' seems to make no attempt to link this creativity with discovery. Like many other commentaries, the article deals with creativity and how to foster it in organisations, assuming, it seems, that if you have creativity you will have discovery. Although Boxenbaum's research is useful, a good follow-on study would have been to explore ways in which creativity could lead to discovery. The same criticism can be directed towards Mullins (1963) who was concerned with the prediction of creativity but seemingly not with the prediction of discovery. Kisiel (1983) writes of the process of discovery in science and claims that it is at least in part a gradual and rational process, but does not relate any of his ideas to the existing research on creativity.

Mansfield and Busse (1981) reach conclusions concerning the developmental antecedents of creative scientists, the creative processes and the personality characteristics of creative scientists. They also make the point that creative scientists should be assessed by what they have produced, rather than by creative tests. Despite the title — *The Psychology of Creativity and Discovery* — however, this book has little to say about discovery.

Inability to generalise across populations

Individuals differ greatly across fields of work and research. With the possible exception of Mullins' (1963) study of a sample of research scientists, few studies on creativity are based on relevant populations for the present study. Samples of undergraduates (e.g. Hocevar, 1980; Runco and Bahleda, 1986; Amabile, Goldfurb and Brackfield, 1990), are not the most valid sample when trying to predict discovery from levels of creativity in eminent scientists. Mansfield and Busse (1981) generalise across all branches of science and also use research carried out on architects and engineers as evidence for some of their arguments. This hardly seems adequate given the differing requirements of each of these occupations.

The studies outlined above (and many others) explore in a number of ingenious ways the relationship between creativity and a variety of other variables, ranging from the sociological to the individual. Detailed studies relating validly measured creativity to substantial, agreed measures of discovery in science simply do not exist. It seems that many researchers see creativity as 'standing for' discovery. However, as we shall see, discovery is a measurable, observable outcome of science research, whereas creativity in scientists, though it may be measurable, has no established relationship with discovery.

The relationship between measured creativity and discovery requires further clarification. It may seem reasonable to expect higher rates of discovery in those scientists with measurably higher levels of creativity. However, this common assumption would need to be established empirically by research. One way of doing this would be to compare samples of scientists who have made substantial discoveries with others who had not, along various measures of creativity. In this way, a possible relationship between creativity and discovery could be explored. This is an example of one of the many exciting pieces of research that needs to be done. Its results would have significant implications, for example, for the selection of scientists.

Extensive though the creativity research is, it would seem that in terms of contributing to our knowledge of the determinants of discovery, it remains incomplete. Even if creativity were shown to be necessary for scientific discovery, creative capacity alone would not appear to be a sufficient characteristic to explain the occurrence of discovery. For extensive surveys of the development of creativity theory, see Taylor and Getsells (1967), Glover, Ronning and Reynolds (1989), Sternberg (1988) and Runco and Albert (1990). The literature abounds with discussions concerning individual creativity and how it is held to lead to 'flashes of insight' which in turn lead to discovery. Many researchers deal with the relationship between creativity and the intelligence and personality of the individual (for an extensive review, see Barron and Harrington, 1981). We are told, for example, that creative individuals, have a wide range of interests (Prentky, 1980; Barron and Harrington, 1981), that they have high levels of intrinsic motivation (Amabile, 1983), that they have a strong belief in their own ideas (Roe, 1953) and that they tend to be more introverted than extroverted (Vernon, 1967). In addition, Parloff *et al.* (1967) describe the creative personality as uninhibited, unconventional, assertive and, self-assured, while having a need for independence, freedom and autonomy. On the intelligence side, some studies have pointed out the importance of divergent thinking in creative individuals (Guilford, 1967b; Chambers, 1969), as well as mental imagery (e.g. Lindauer, 1977) and the ability to form unusual associations (MacKinnon, 1962; Gough, 1976). As a consequence of this kind of thinking, much effort has been directed towards developing tests to identify creative individuals (e.g. Torrance, 1966).

Interesting as these studies are, they seem to give the impression that because individuals differ in terms of creativity, it is always better for a research laboratory or university to have creative people in all areas. However, it is indeed possible that a person may be highly creative but lack the additional qualities of personality and character necessary to produce a creative output such as a major discovery. Direct links between high creativity in individual scientists and substantial acknowledged discovery have not been established.

In one study of the concurrent validity of selected subtests of Torrance tests of creative thinking among individuals at high levels of recognition in art and science, Kanter (1984) found that 'the tests were not effective in identifying the most creative artists or scientists'. According to Kanter, the results give a profile of the creative person as one who expresses ideas simply, whose thinking tends to stick to a problem area and who can think rapidly. Persistence seems to be as important as high scores on creativity tests.

Lack of an adequate criterion for genius/creative person

If one presumes for the moment that creativity in the scientific individual is a highly desirable trait for the research laboratory, the next area that needs to be addressed is the establishment of meaningful criteria for creativity. According to Boxenbaum (1991, p. 476) scientific creativity can be divided into the 'consensual' and 'conceptual' perspective:

> From the consensual perspective, a scientific activity is creative to the extent that an appropriate panel of experts independently and subjectively agree to its creativity. From the conceptual standpoint, a scientific activity is deemed to be creative to the extent that (a) it is both novel and relevant to the task at hand, and (b) the task is heuristic rather than algorithmic; that is, the task does not rely on a clear and readily identifiable path to its solution.

Many articles on the creative individual or 'the genius mind' (Briggs, 1984) rely heavily on evaluation and publications as determinants of creative output. It appears to be accepted that if a group of people agree that an individual is a creative genius, we should not question their opinion. Ryhammar and Brolin (1991) argue, however, that in the past authors have been too quick to equate eminence and productivity with creativity. Clement (1988) attempted to develop predictive measures of research productivity among a sample of PhD recipients. The study made use of a weighting system of frequency of publications in sociology journals called the Glenn–Villemez comprehensive index, or GVCI (Glenn and Villemez, 1970). As Clement acknowledges, however, the GVCI measures only the quantity, not the quality, of publications (see also Cole and Cole, 1967). Clearly, a publication does not always signify a significant contribution to science, nor is it always illustrative of creative talent. Cole and Cole (1967) dealt with this issue when examining the reward system in science. Specifically, the study examined the relationship between the quality and quantity of research produced by scientists. Quality in this case was assessed by the frequency of citations, and this was also done by means of a weighting system depending on how soon after the original work that the author was cited. Although previous research (e.g. Clark 1957) has concluded that citations are the best available method of assessing the quality of published research, its reliability has not been established. Therefore it is difficult for the present study to draw any meaningful conclusions from previous research.

Creative potential versus creative output

When it comes to measuring creative ability and potential, there seems to be an apparent unwillingness to accept that there is a huge difference between potential and output. Sternberg and Lubart (1992) draw attention to this point in their 'investment theory' of creativity. Potential is usually measured by means of a creative ability test. Examples of these tests include the remote associates test (Mednick, 1962, 1963), the unusual uses test (Guilford *et al.*, 1956) and Torrance's test battery for children (Torrance, 1974). However, if this potential never translates into a significant contribution to science, the creative ability test is not of much use in selection. Garfield (1970) claimed that one could predict the most likely recipients of the Nobel Prize in science based on the number and frequency of citations and Zuckermann (1967) drew attention to the productive frequency and longevity of eminent scientists. While there are readily observable examples of these claims, they cannot be a reliable predictor of success. For example, if we observe that all Nobel laureates have over two hundred publications to their credit, we cannot say that all scientists with the same number of publications will win the Nobel Prize. Nevertheless, at least these studies recognise the importance of being able to observe the creative product. Furthermore, they recognise the important distinction between creative potential and the outcome of that potential.

Albert and Runco (1989) examined whether or not there was a possible link between independence and creative potential in young gifted boys. For the purposes of the present study, however, this research cannot be of use because there is no way of knowing whether or not the potential in young boys (however gifted) will translate into a significant scientific output. Methodologically also, one simply cannot generalise across populations (i.e. from gifted boys to eminent scientists). Furthermore, the independent variable was measured by the ratings of mothers of gifted boys as well as the subjects themselves. Ratings are, by their very nature, subjective opinions which will vary from person to person. In Mullins' (1963) sample of research scientists, for example, none of the subjects was rated by more than one supervisor. In a number of other studies, creativity among scientists has been measured using peer evaluation and the number of publications. The latter method is clearly unreliable, since the quality of publications varies widely depending on the particular journal. Lipetz (1965), in an attempt to grapple with this question of quality and objectivity, suggests that:

> In measuring the scientific content of research communications, the basic procedures are (1) to recognize occurrences in novel or original form of the six concepts which represent scientific achievement (description, explanation, definition, hypothesis, prediction, and experimental method) and (2) to count these occurrences. The result of applying these basic procedures is a series of simple totals, one for each type of concept; these totals represent the scientific content of the communications from which they are derived.

The strong emphasis on the creative individual, and indeed our fascination with such people, has obscured a range of other factors including organisational factors, which may play an important part in the discovery process.

The interactionist perspective (Woodman and Schoenfeldt, 1990) recognises the role of social influences on the individual. However, models such as these tend to ignore the possibility that creativity in the individual may not be as important as the organisational conditions that lead to the product of creativity (i.e. discovery). In other words, creativity may not occur within the person at all, but rather as a result of the accumulation of knowledge from many different sources and the collaboration of large numbers of scientists.

One of the few authors to make reference to the importance of the organisation was Andrews (1967) in a study of creative ability in the laboratory environment. This study compared how universities, industrial firms and government laboratories effect creative ability and performance. Ability was measured by the remote association test (Mednick, 1963), while performance was measured by self-report and evaluations of others. Andrews found that creative ability on its own was an ineffective measure of scientific achievement. Rather, ability was seen to influence performance only when other factors were taken into account. These factors included:

(a) Time spent in a certain area. (Creative ability influences performance if the scientist is involved in the area for a short period of time. This applied also to the length of time spent on a project.)
(b) Co-ordination in the group. (If the co-ordination was tight, creative ability depressed performance, whereas loose co-ordination meant that creative ability either helped or had no effect on performance.)
(c) The quality of communication of ideas would affect whether or not they are translated into performance.
(d) The reward system must value creativity rather than well-established methods.

This study was important because of its many organisational implications. For example, it was observed that the goals of research should not be so rigid that they stifle creativity, reward systems should encourage creativity and communication of ideas should be ensured. In other words, the remote associations test may show that an individual has creative potential, but no discovery will result without these organisational factors. However, the measures of scientific performance in this research do not seem adequate because self-reports involved only the quantity of publications, while the evaluations of others were open to subjective bias.

Amabile (1983) examined the role of evaluation systems, training and modelling in relation to creative behaviour. These ideas, however, seem to deal more with the effect of innovation on the organisation than the effect of the organisation on creativity. The distinction between innovation and creativity is an important one. West and Farr (1990) point out that creativity is concerned with the generation of ideas whereas innovation refers more to their application. The Amabile study refers to innovation only, not to discovery. The much needed examination of organisational factors accounting for differences in individual creativity is the first step towards a more holistic view of the phenomenon. The next is to determine how useful creativity is in terms of scientific performance.

4   CHARACTERISTICS NEEDED FOR CREATIVITY

Curiosity and discovery

What we do know from scientists of distinction is that their personalities and characters play important parts in their discoveries. They must have exceptional curiosity; Asimov (1984) tells us in virtually biblical tones: 'Almost in the beginning was curiosity.' This curiosity is not of the idle kind that goes away when finding out becomes difficult. It is rather of a very persistent nature, allowing no obstacle to deter them from the insight into nature that they seek. Richard Ernst tells us:

> I found that I was motivated initially by an innate curiosity about the mysteries of nature. Later, however, it was a desire to achieve something.

Discovery is the result of a long process, driven by curiosity, of hypothesis generation, experimentation, refinement of thinking, and further experimentation. After many years of patient persistent research, a few scientists are rewarded with the excitement of some new scientific discovery, and experience the thrill of intellectual achievement. Earlier frustrations lose their baleful impact on the minds of those who have suffered them. This long, patient, process of persistent inquiry may often be easily forgotten by the world at large, and even, perhaps, by those who themselves have achieved substantial discovery. Reiser (1971) puts it this way:

> True creativity in research requires, in addition that a man be driven, even obsessed, by a compelling sense of curiosity (hopefully combined with the ability to ask researchable questions). Curiosity as a trait is so fundamental a requirement that it surely warrants the development of sensitive and sophisticated methods for its assessment, and special methods for its nurturance.

Taylor takes a view that creativity in science is the name people put on successful thinking:

> This whole thing of creativity really gives *thinking* a bad name; I mean most of the things you call creative, are just doing things right, and then being faced with something that forces you to be creative.

For Taylor, the interest in science, the curiosity about nature, is the primary source of scientific insight.

Motivation and discovery

Motivation is central to intellectual effort. A distinction must be made, however, between motivation that arises from the task itself (intrinsic motivation) and motivation that comes from money, or some other reward (extrinsic motivation). Most psychologists take the view that intrinsic motivation is more important than extrinsic motivation, in relation to work productivity (Amabile, 1983). Amabile puts forward the view that 'intrinsic motivation to do the task' is an essential part of the creative process. She sees it as one of three components at the individual level which shape the creative individual, the other two being skills in the task domain and skills in the creative thinking (see Figure 7).

1 **Domain-relevant skills**	2 **Creativity-relevant skills**	3 **Task motivation**
Includes: – Knowledge about the domain – Technical skills required – Special domain-relevant 'talent' *Depends on:* – Innate cognitive abilities – Innate perceptual and motor skills – Formal and informal education	*Includes:* – Appropriate cognitive style – Implicit or explicit knowledge of heuristics for generating novel ideas – Conductive work style *Depends on:* – Training – Experience in idea generation – Personality characteristics	*Includes:* – Attitudes towards the task – Perceptions of own motivation for undertaking the task *Depends on:* – Initial level of intrinsic motivation toward the task – Presence or absence of salient extrinsic constraints in the social environment – Individual ability to cognitively minimize extrinsic constraints

Figure 7 Amabile's 'componential model of individual creativity'. From JPSP, 1983, **45**, p. 362. Copyright © 1983 by the American Psychological Association. Reprinted with permission

Very few studies exist of the precise ways by which the organisational environment affects creativity in science, and none at all as to how it might affect discovery. Some studies exist that do approach the creative aspects of science, including those of Taylor and Sandler (1973), Ekvall and Tangberg-Andersson (1986) and Amabile (1988). These studies show results that highlight the importance of the following in encouraging creativity:

(a) freedom, unexpected rewards, good project management,
(b) positive climate of innovation, stimulating physical milieu,
(c) scope for playfulness and security of employment.

Factors that they found to inhibit creativity include:

(a) limited freedom of choice, expected rewards, pressure of evaluation, pressure from peers and pressure from being supervised.

Another theory of motivation which may have particular reference to science research is that of Sternberg and Lubart (1992). The 'investment theory', as they call it, assumes that as in financial dealings where people buy low and sell high so in the choice of research projects creative people will wish to choose topics that are neither fashionable, nor developed, because in these they can make the greatest progress.

Motivation in relation to tasks such as science research can be measured. Not all scientists can be assumed to have the levels of quasi-obsessive motivation required to make discoveries. Motivation studies have (in areas other than science) discovered a number of correlates of motivation towards the task. Locke (1968) showed that setting hard goals resulted in higher performance and that setting very specific hard goals was more motivating than a 'do your best' approach. Maslow (1943) proposed a hierarchy of motivations, such that the lower needs had to be satisfied before a higher one became a motivator. Thus our need for food and safety comes before our need to socialise. The highest need postulated by Maslow was for self-actualisation. In Maslow's (1943, p. 377) seminal article proposing this theory, he makes specific reference to scientific curiosity as bridging several of his levels of motivation:

> Acquiring knowledge and systematizing the universe have been considered as in part, techniques for the achievement of basic safety in the world, or for the intelligent man, expressions of self actualization.

Expectancy theory (Vroom, 1964) is another theory that may have special possibilities for science research. This theory puts forward the idea that individuals assign probability levels and values to outcomes of their work, and in effect become highly motivated if there is a high probability of a satisfactory outcome for a valued area of their work. For scientists working in basic research, motivational levels must remain high even when the probability of successful outcomes is low. This suggests that their work might best be structured in batches of achievable objectives, all of which are directed towards the larger objective of discovery. No research has been carried out on this.

Many motivation theories refer to organisational factors external to the individual as relatively unimportant in terms of motivating people. What seems to be agreed among theorists in this area is that individual intrapsychic processes are much more powerful as motivators. Herzberg identified the nature of the work itself, Maslow the need for the individual to move through certain developmental stages and McClelland identified a personal need for achievement. More recently Weiner (1985) has put forward a theory whose central core lies in the attempt by individuals to seek to discover why events occur and to attribute causes for those occurrences. There are five causal dimensions to Weiner's theory; these are 'locus of control', 'temporal stability', 'cross-situational generality', 'controllability' and 'intentionality' (Robertson, Cooper and Smith, 1992).

People with high levels of 'locus of control' do not see themselves as pawns in some game, but rather as in charge and responsible for most aspects of their lives. Those with high 'temporal stability' see their abilities as relatively stable over time, and therefore a source of constant support to them in their intellectual efforts. Those with 'cross-situational generality' see their abilities as capable of application in a wide variety of situations. Those with high 'controllability', in Weiner's terms, regard themselves as largely in control of the amount of effort they expend on chosen activities. This is very much the opposite of those who see themselves as having learned to be helpless or who see others as the prime movers in relation to their work. Those who have high levels of 'intentionality' are more likely to 'initiate action', in Heckhausen's (1991) terms.

This theory of human motivation explores in a very detailed way minute but centrally important aspects of motivation. It seems to fit better with the world of the scientist than most others, in that the scientist has high freedom and independence needs. The higher these needs, the more original is his or her mind. In De Charms' terms, the discoverer-scientist is 'an origin, not a pawn' (De Charms, 1968). Such an original scientist is one of exceptional ability, and is aware as a result of years of academic feedback that they possess superior scientific aptitudes. Such individuals have what Bandura (1977, 1986, 1991) refers to as 'high self-efficacy'. Self-efficacy is described by Gist and Mitchell (1992) as: 'a person's belief about his or her capabilities to perform a task'.

The locus of control of events of those with high self-efficacy lies within themselves, and they are spurred on to greater efforts by apparent obstacles. Novelty and the unknown are seen as stimuli, rather than threats. This sense of internal control and potential is a characteristic of individuals high in self-efficacy and of the Nobel laureates in this study. It is likely, then, that the link between freedom and motivation is through control and self-efficacy. This could tentatively be modelled as shown in Figure 8.

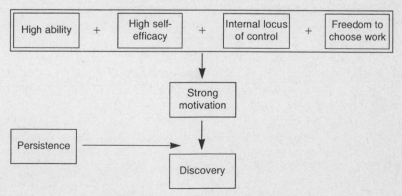

Figure 8   The motivation to discover

The high-ability scientist, who also has high levels of self-efficacy and a high internal locus of control, is likely to be highly motivated. If this person also has strong persistence, the discovery is more likely than in other scientists where all or some of these variables are weak or absent. This is of course a probabilistic statement, since one cannot say with absolute certainty that such a person, modelled above, will definitely discover something new and important. However, this process all takes place within an organisation, and is assisted by the investigator's own organisational skills.

Persistence and discovery

It is interesting that none of the Nobel laureates in the present study described themselves as being particularly creative. Instead, they emphasised the importance of persistence, a compendious knowledge of the literature and related literature, and hard work. Rohrer describes himself as follows:

> Maybe we should be clear of one thing; what my creativity is. I think I am not a creative person in that I have abundant ideas. I discard a lot of ideas while I am thinking about them. My contribution to creativity is I think recognising something which can be important, but not making or inventing the important thing myself. That is how I see my contribution to many things.

Persistence, too, is highlighted by Ericsson, Krampe and Tesch-Romer (1993). This study concludes that deliberate practice has an influential role creating a persistent personality, and hence to influence expert performance.

Worthley (1992) found that persistence in science is strongly related to values. The values of care for others, which science might relate to an attempt to find a cure for some disease, or a justice perspective, which relates to 'rights, rules, objectivity and autonomy in making choices', both play a key role in determining a scientist's tendency to persist in the solution of some difficult task. Richard Ernst tells us:

> You have to combine a questioning of everything with a will to achieve something.

Certainly the history of discovery science is full of evidence of persistence. Einstein after many years of work produced his special theory of relativity in 1905; it was not until 1916 that he published his general theory; and he spent the rest of his life trying to develop a theory which would explain in a unified way all the physical forces of nature.

Hewish describes his early work in the Cavendish:

> I was engaged on other projects to begin with, designing and making antennas for surveys of radio galaxies. I spent a lot of time hacking my way through piles of brass tubing and so forth, making antennas; I mean it was real sweat and toil and a lot of time in gum boots. You built all the apparatus yourself those days, you know, you didn't call in contractors to do it and I spent half my time getting soaked to the skin about a mile from here in the observatory setting up antennas in

the rain and all that. But research projects gradually emerge. It's an apprenticeship as a research student and certainly in those days you joined the group and you got used to the way they operated and then after a while your own project would become clear. I was just joining the team when I began. But then, there was this business about the radio sources fluctuating. Was this caused by the ionosphere or was it caused by the source itself, intrinsic fluctuations?

Immense persistence in this very physical activity preceded any clarity of theory in this matter, and Hewish had the ability, the curiosity and the persistence to stick with this problem and, in spite of the hard work involved, to be able to think though the problem to its successful conclusion.

Knowledge of their field in science

It would not be accurate to assume that every scientist is equally well prepared. The education of scientists differs greatly from country to country, and also within countries. A considerable amount of research has been carried out by sociologists interested in science. Those studies including work by Cole and Cole (1967), Merton (1973) and Zuckermann (1967) have shown that social factors have strong effects on science. Other sociologists including Latour (1987) have shown the place of laboratory work within its broader social context.

However, in spite of current trends to try to measure everything that moves in research, there is a singular absence of objective data on the quality of the educational experience. Some aspects of this experience are measurable: the number of hours taught, the number of faculty with PhDs, the number of publications per faculty member, per student for example. Others, such as the infectious enthusiasm of a lecturer for his or her subject, or their interest in fostering and mentoring students of particular promise, are probably not measurable. Nevertheless, the general point here is that we cannot assume that each science graduate has had a similar preparation for their work in research. We shall see in Chapter 4, that Crane (1965) has shown a strong effect on publication rate, depending on whether the scientist attended a major or a minor university.

5   WHY DOES THE INDIVIDUAL SCIENTIST NEED ORGANISATION?

Though it is clear that the individual scientist is paramount in all research, yet the scientist works embedded in the group, social and organisational structure of a laboratory. Science is a social matter and requires substantial resources to be effective.

We might imagine identical twins, reared together and, having pursued a scientific career, achieving doctoral degrees in similar areas of the natural sciences. One enters the Harvard Chemistry Department where Dudley Herschbach is his colleague. He has two hours teaching during one semester and is part of a research team working in an area of interest to him. The research is generously funded and the department is rich in exceptional colleagues, technical support and the requisite equipment.

The other twin enters a respectable but undistinguished university chemistry department, where the average number of publications per staff member is two. He is given ten hours per week lecturing all year, the research budget is tiny, and support of various kinds is thin. Assuming identical abilities and motivation, it would seem reasonable to suggest that twin number one may make substantial achievements in his research while twin number two will not, the only difference being the level of organisational resources.

Of course, the second twin, being identical, would probably move out of the undistinguished university as soon as it were possible, and over time might achieve as much as his twin. However, the general point that resources are an important factor is illustrated by this imaginary example.

Our attention, then, is directed towards the nature of this scientific organisation and the degree to which it contributes to the incidence of discovery in science. The most important point to be stressed here is that nowadays most scientists (including all those Nobel laureates in the present study) work in organisations. If we exclude those most exclusively introspective sciences such as mathematics and theoretical physics, it is clear that laboratory-based science needs laboratories. Laboratories are located in larger organisations such as research institutes or universities. Yet many scientists are sceptical of organisation. In Elion's view:

> Organisation to me has a bad connotation; it often means that the person at the top doesn't understand the scientific process.

Elion's scepticism of organisations is probably shared by most scientists. However, we need to know very much more about the nature of scientific organisations that facilitate discovery. Although we have a fair knowledge of the characteristics of scientists, their abilities, their performance on tests and examinations, their social antecedents, attitudes, etc., we also know quite a lot about the nature of each scientific discovery. What we know surprisingly little about is the nature of the organisational circumstances that prevail in laboratories and their surrounding parent organisations. This is true whether they be laboratories where discovery takes place or not. Among the areas where we have little knowledge are the structure of the parent organisation and its relationship to the laboratory, the organisational structure within the laboratories, supervisory styles and practices, the prevailing selection practices, the scientific approaches taken and the resources available. We also know very little about the organisational (as distinct from scientific) skills of the discoverer-scientist.

Throughout history, some individuals have had a strong desire to know, to probe deeply and to speculate. Science has always been an absorbing activity and requires a lot from those involved, both personally and as members of scientific groups. The field of organisation theory and practice is a much more widespread one, applied in a variety of differing settings. Because of the scarcity of studies linking organisation specifically with science, it is not yet clear how organisation, other than the personal organising ability of the principal investigator, can help in science research. Many feel that those who are responsible for organising have the organisation as a priority, not the aims of the scientific projects that make up the very purpose of that organisation. As a result, a number of scientists remain convinced that the only good organisation is that which they themselves as principal investigators control.

This is not a new phenomenon. In antiquity and in the Middle Ages, scientists were wealthy people or had wealthy patrons. This access to wealth gave them the freedom from most other concerns, which was necessary to allow them to devote themselves to speculation and inquiry. As well as freedom, however, substantial resources of many kinds were needed. These resources most frequently took the form of servants carrying out aspects of their investigations, and seeking new or additional information. However, the principal investigator was always in control of the studies that took place.

Modern scientists, though not usually wealthy, are similar in many ways. Like their predecessors, they are driven by a consuming interest in a focused area of the natural world. They are similar, too, in their general approach to scientific problems: they have a very clear understanding of the nature of the problem, they define terms clearly, think logically and devise experiments to test their theories.

However, important differences do exist. In modern science, the scale, the technology and the information processing requirements are of a magnitude much greater than in earlier times. One has only to consider Boyle's experiments which show 'the spring in the air' and contrast these homely projects with the scale of experimental plant in CERN and SLAC, for example, to realise the extraordinary scale and technology involved in this area of science. In these cases, huge installations of plant and equipment are needed to expand our knowledge of particle physics. Complex technological support is also needed in areas such as medicine, biology and engineering, and in many other areas of science.

It could be argued that there is an organisational implication of this much greater scale and complexity. It is possible that much science can no longer be carried out by one dedicated person with personally organised support. Hence the research laboratory and its associated wider organisation is replacing the earlier patronage system in making discovery possible.

The organisations that carry out these functions today are usually either universities or research laboratories. In both cases, they must have access to very considerable funding. This funding enables them to maintain organisational systems to support the scientist in creative exploration. Accordingly, this organisational support, in terms of personnel services, fund-raising, financial management, buildings administration and technical support, should provide a background which enables the scientist to create his or her own scientific organisation, the purpose of which is to experiment and to explore, to measure and hypothesise.

Descriptions of scientific discovery throughout the ages have mainly been descriptions of the development of ideas and of the thinking processes involved — from Boyle's experiments with mercury and glass tubes to measure the active power of air to resist compression, and thus explain why 'nature abhors a vacuum'; to Lavoisier's experimental isolation of oxygen from mercuric oxide and recognition that Priestley's 'phlogisticated' air was simply air with the oxygen removed; to Darwin's proposal, based on fossil evidence and biogeography, of the mutability of species and the importance of natural selection; to Pasteur's contribution to the modern conception of disease by showing that diseases resulted from attacks of micro-organisms, and that these micro-organisms do not arise from spontaneous generation and by pioneering the preparation of artificial vaccines; to J. J. Thomson's measurement of the mass-to-charge ratio of cathode rays in evacuated tubes by comparing deflection due to electric and magnetic fields, which led to the discovery of the electron when it was found that this ratio was independent of the nature of the gas used to generate the cathode rays; to Rutherford's experiments which prompted the novel hypothesis that radioactive rays given off by a substance are due to the disintegration of the atoms into a new substance (Harre, 1981). All of these great experiments are histories of the development of ideas and theoretical explanations.

Yet these histories of experiments and ideas omit the importance of the resources that made the research possible. A number of examples of this are evident. Boyle's studies owed much to the founding of the Royal Society, which was instrumental in defining the 'experimental space' of modern science (Shapin and Schaffer, 1985). Lavoisier was helped greatly by the invaluable English to French and French to English translations made by Lavoisier's wife which facilitated his competition with Priestley (Harre, 1981). Darwin's political skill and successful exploitation of the social structure of British and American science allowed his seemingly heretical theories to get a fair hearing (Kitcher, 1993). Pasteur's cultivation of financial resources, his intellectual migration from the study of the optical activity of asymmetric molecules, to the mechanism of fermentation, and the cause and prevention of diseases, as well as his reliance on a team of assistants to continue his work after he suffered a stroke, were vital. J. J. Thomson's building of a powerful research school whose influence extended throughout the British Empire and his involvement with the founding and advising of the Department of Scientific and Industrial Research allowed his own research to progress. Finally, Rutherford's training by J. J. Thomson and his fruitful collaborations with Frederick Soddy, with Geiger and Marsden and with Niels Bohr were significant contributors to his success (Harre, 1981). These are important examples of the organisational roles played by some outstanding scientists in recent times.

However, all these rich and diverse personal characteristics, though absolutely necessary for the discoverer-scientist, are unlikely to be sufficient for discovery to become a fact. Gould (1996), writing about the reasons for Charles Darwin contributing so much to science, gives as his view:

> All the world's brilliance, and all the souls energy, cannot combine to produce historical impact without a happy coincidence of external factors that cannot be fully controlled: the health and peace required to live into adulthood; sufficient social acceptability to gain a hearing; and life in a century able to understand (though not necessarily at least at first to believe).

These 'external factors' are the subject of the rest of this book.

Chapter 4

The Eminent Scientists and their Organisations

1 INTRODUCTION

When it was decided to carry out this study, the author wrote to all 160 living Nobel laureates asking them to take part. Sixteen agreed to take part, and many of the remainder wrote strongly encouraging letters of support for the project. Several sent books and articles to provide useful additional information.*

The interviews took place during 1993–1994, and the questionnaires were administered in 1994. Once the interview series started, the author was impressed with the willingness and enthusiasm of the Laureates to contribute to this study, and hopefully to our understanding of the processes leading to scientific discovery. It became clear very quickly that this enthusiasm was an important personal characteristic which had contributed significantly to their own work. In fact their enthusiasm coupled with their persistence in dogged pursuit of the secrets of nature struck this writer as something wholly exceptional, and probably of great significance in their work in science. Their enthusiasm seemed very close to the Greek meaning of the word: 'possession by a god'. This enthusiasm undoubtedly led to their compendious knowledge of their own field (and several others). Whether this enthusiasm, or this

---

*The Nobel laureates who have been interviewed are: (1) Frederick Sanger (two Nobel Prizes), University of Cambridge, (2) Anthony Hewish, University of Cambridge, (3) Geoffrey Wilkinson, Imperial College London, (4) Abdus Salam, Institute of Theoretical Physics, (5) Simon van der Meer, CERN, Geneva, (6) Heinrich Rohrer, IBM Research Centre, Zurich, (7) Richard Ernst, ETH, Zurich, (8) Vladimir Prelog, ETH, Zurich, (9) Herbert Brown, Purdue University, (10) Baruj Bennacerrif, Dana-Farber Cancer Institute, Boston, (11) Baruch Blumberg, Fox Chase Cancer Center, Pa., (12) Herbert Hauptman, Buffalo Medical Centre (13) Dudley Herschbach, Harvard University, (14) George Hitchings, Wellcome Research Laboratories, N.C., (15) Gertrude Elion, Wellcome Research Laboratories, N.C., (16) Richard Taylor, Stanford Linear Accelerator.

persistence, was the decisive factor leading to their substantial contributions to science, or whether they were factors among many others, is not clear.

They seemed also to have an unusually unclouded and articulate understanding of the nature of problems in their area of science. This could be taken to be '*post hoc* rationalization' were it not for the fact that many of them had displayed this clarity as to the nature of the problems when they were young people, long before honours had come their way, or even before they had worked in science in any substantial way. Wilkinson, for example, as a 25 year old looked at the given structure of a metal–butadiene compound and knew it was wrong. Knew it was wrong! he had no doubts, he knew it was wrong! Elion, too, as a young girl, after losing some of her dearest relatives to cancer, knew that a cure for cancer was a possibility.

When it came to the precise scientific problems to be addressed they all seemed to know pretty much what needed to be done, and how to go about it! Their own personal capacity as organisers and leaders was very clear. They have both the authoritative vision to guide their research and the charisma to imbue others with a desire to collaborate in their research. These extensive and admirable personal characteristics might blind us to the fact that they all chose and valued the support of generously endowed and resourced organisations, in which they carried out their seminal work. This chapter introduces the sixteen eminent scientists, describes some of their projects, emphasising the organisational skills needed to carry them out successfully, and describes the resources available in the organisations in which they worked.

2   THE EMINENT SCIENTISTS

Frederick Sanger won the 1958 Nobel Prize in Chemistry for his determination of the complete chemical structure of insulin. This work is a landmark in biochemistry, because it showed for the first time that a protein has a precisely defined amino acid sequence. It stimulated other scientists to carry out sequence studies of a wide variety of proteins. Indeed, the complete amino acid sequences of more than 10 000 proteins are now known. He won another Nobel Prize in Chemistry in 1980 for his role in developing a method to determine base sequences in nucleic acids. This accomplishment revealed the total information content of a DNA genome.

Sanger was born in Redcomb, Gloucestershire, England, on 13 August, 1918. He attended Cambridge University, where he received his BA in Natural Sciences in 1940 and his PhD in 1943. As a Quaker and conscientious objector, Sanger was able to continue his education uninterrupted during wartime. Beginning in 1944, Sanger taught at Cambridge, where he has spent his entire professional career. Sanger's friendship with his Cambridge colleague Francis Crick helped him develop an interest in genetics when protein sequencing began to seem too routine. The lectures Sanger received from Crick and coworkers on genetics facilitated the studies that led to his second Nobel Prize. His work has made possible a current major scientific goal, the sequencing of the entire human genome, which contains 3.5×109 pairs.

During our interview, the question of whether the organisation surrounding the research, the colleagues or some unique individual trait was central to making discovery possible, arose. Sanger commented:

> I gradually built up a (research) group in the biochemistry. Biochemistry took place in a teaching lab and though most of the people were on the staff of the biochemical lab, they were more concerned with teaching. Now I have tried to avoid teaching all the time, and I managed to do so. I suppose because none of my work in that area was very good. I then got a medical research fellowship which was fairly prestigious and did enable you to do exactly what you liked. I held that for 27 years and that gave me freedom. I had a fairly easy time and I didn't have to teach, which I didn't want to do. I might have got into the teaching line but I never did and that helped I think because I could afford to spend my full time there. There were other people in the lab who were very helpful to me and I could always discuss things with them. That was another thing that working in the lab enabled one to do. The lab was the leading biochemistry lab in the country and you got very good students. These were post-doctoral people and they would come and talk to you, and I found that usually one got more out of talking to the younger research people than from more senior people.

On the organisation in his laboratory he said:

> Well the organization was fairly good, but I was completely free to do research at that time; but I think the problem you see was one which appealed to me particularly. You see, at that time there were no sequences developed and yet sequences play a very important part in biology. Things like, even now, human gender projects, you should be reading the whole sequences of the genes and as a basis really for human understanding and working and I think I realized this perhaps more than most people. That sequences really were the important thing and they were all messages, I think. So I really went all out for it. There were very few people who worked on it or had. It was something that had not been known. Nobody had done anything and I was able to develop methods and actually came up with the complete sequence of insulin which was a big breakthrough.

Herbert C. Brown won the Nobel Prize in Chemistry in 1979 for his discovery and exploration of borohydrides and organoboranes, which revolutionized the field of organic synthesis. Brown was born in London, England, on 22 May 1912 and emigrated to Chicago, Illinois, USA, while a young boy. He received his AS from Wright Junior College (Illinois) in 1935. He then attended the University of Chicago, where he received his BS in 1936 and his PhD in 1938.

Brown taught at the University of Chicago from 1940 to 1943 and at Wayne State University (Michigan) from 1943 to 1947, before finally settling at Purdue University. Brown was a professor at Purdue from 1947 to 1978 and, since 'retiring', has continued to support an active research group of postdoctoral fellows and to publish extensively. Throughout his very active career he has been a prolific author in the chemical literature and his work continues to be extensively cited and applied to the solution of problems in synthetic organic chemistry. In addition to his work with organoboranes, Brown has been extensively involved with developments in other areas of chemistry. Amongst these have been major contributions to physical organic chemistry, including steric effects, quantitative approaches to the study of aromatic substitution processes, the introduction of σ^+ constants as an aid to understanding the influence of substituents on chemical reactivity and the 'non-classical' carbonium ion controversy. More recently he has been applying organoborane methodology to the solution of problems in enantioselective synthesis, one of the most fundamentally important and active areas in modern synthetic chemistry.

In his interview with the present author, when asked about his general approach to scientific problem-solving, he said:

> We found solutions to problems and made them work. Why did we achieve this? One, I have a very good knowledge of chemistry, I retain that knowledge and I can recall the factor that will fit the given situation to give us a hopeful plan. The second thing as I told you, I am not content with merely solving a problem, I always want to explore the area, so I end up knowing all the chemistry involved for these compounds.

Was his scientific success due entirely to himself or to his scientific team? He gave his view:

> Both. I think first you have got to have capable people who are willing to listen to you and to follow it down; if they are not competent, they will always go around making mistakes and you will spend all your time correcting these mistakes. But I think you must then take responsibility for selecting people who are competent, or training them to be competent.

He also noted:

> I have observed that the best chemists are those who speak and write very clearly. When I get their graduate records in, the most important score there is the language one (the verbal score); the chemistry results, or the quantitative one, is of secondary importance to me. Invariably, I have found that the people who have the qualities of the mind that allow people to formulate the language to express things clearly are able to formulate research and do it in a systematic excellent manner.

When it was pointed out that, many people would find it unusual to say that verbal skills are important in selecting a chemist rather than taking somebody with good technical and quantitative skills, he gave it as his view that:

> I think you first need the intelligence. I think the intelligence of handling the English language is related to the ability to do first rate research. ... At Purdue, we have about three hundred registered students working there and we keep excellent

records for many years. Invariably, we have gone back and compared whom we think are the best chemists we have turned out and compared these with their graduate exam records. We find no correlation with their grades, no correlation with their undergraduate grades, no correlation with their chemistry graduate exam or their quantitative skills, but quite a good correlation with their verbal scores.

Richard Ernst was born in Winterthur, Switzerland, in 1933. He graduated with a degree in chemical engineering from the Swiss Federal Institute of Technology in Zurich and proceeded to complete his doctoral work with Hans Primas in the area of nuclear magnetic resonance (NMR). After graduating he joined Varian Laboratories in California and worked with others, including Weston Anderson, on the development of NMR technology towards a commercial goal. He was awarded the Nobel Prize in Physics in 1991.

When I asked him how he got his scientific ideas he said:

> For finding a solution to a posed problem, it is important to think about it intensively, do the necessary calculations and identify yourself completely with the problem. Then stop and do something completely different for a while, relax, and think about something (or somebody) you like, and suddenly the solution you were searching for is here! It is like trying to remember names of people. You may think as hard as possible without any success, and then later suddenly the name comes to your mind. Often, I am working for half-an-hour at my desk, then I walk around or leaning back and looking into the blue sky for 10 minutes, and suddenly the solution comes to my mind. Brainstorming with a group of people is inspiring, but to find a valid solution one needs afterwards a quiet atmosphere to collect one's thoughts and perhaps luckily have a great idea.

When I explored this with him further, surprised by his apparent lack of involvement with others in developing his ideas, I asked him whether the existence of colleagues, and discussions with them, stimulated his ideas by example. He replied:

> It is certainly inspiring to learn about the creativity of other scientists. What others can do, one hopes to be able to achieve oneself. Other scientists provide measures for oneself and a healthy feeling of competition occurs that stimulates one's own creativity. It is very important to work in an environment of excellence to mobilize all one's gifts and possibilities.

Vladimir Prelog was awarded the Nobel Prize in 1975 for his work on chirality in chemistry. He discovered many novel types of chiral chemicals and though this work, commenced with a deep interest in chemical structures and the relationship of structure to function, his synthesis of chiral forms led him to a preoccupation with specifying the growing numbers of stereoisomers of organic compounds. The CIP (Cahn–Ingold–Prelog) was developed for defining absolute configuration using sequence rules.

In describing his approach to research he said:

> I was fascinated by chemistry, by compounds, by making something which nobody had seen before, nobody had investigated before. To see even the reaction which

we had planned not go the way we wanted it to, but result in something entirely different and surprising.

The use of Prelog's system of assigning R or S to stereogenic centres, axes and planes is ubiquitous. It is impossible to find papers published today, which involve stereochemistry, that do not use this system. The system is so widely accepted that there is a continuous conversion from the previous definition of chiral centres, the L and D system (based on glyceraldehyde), to Prelog's. For example, many authors will now use R and S for the chiral centres of amino acids, the bastion of the L and D system. This simple and practical procedure for defining stereochemistry has allowed chemists to talk fluently with one another with respect to chirality.

Simon van der Meer was born in the Netherlands in 1925 and graduated as an engineer from the University of Delft in 1952. He started his scientific career with Philips in Eindhoven and moved in 1962 to CERN in Geneva, where he and colleagues J. B. Adams and C. A. Ramm were occupied with the construction of the synchrotron. His early pioneering work centred around stochastic cooling and the accumulation of antiprotons, for which he received the Nobel Prize in 1984.

We discussed the nature of ideas and their essentially revolutionary nature. He said:

I would agree that an important factor in a creative scientist is an interest in attacking existing theories. The main interest, however, is in looking at something with a purpose—being able to do something that you need for something else.

His ideas often came to him by surprise, in relaxed moments when he was not aware of thinking about his physics problems:

I had many of my ideas at home in the evening before going to sleep. Usually when you are not forced to do anything in particular you think of things. The mind has to be free for thinking about things and you have to have a randomish way of thinking.

Abdus Salam shared the 1979 Nobel Prize in Physics for contributing to the theory of unified weak and electromagnetic interaction between elementary particles, a major step towards an overall unified field theory. Salam was born in Jhang, Pakistan on 29 January 1926. He attended the University of Punjab, where he received his MA in 1946. Salam then attended Cambridge University, where he received a BA in 1948, a PhD in 1952 and a DSc in 1957.

In 1951, Salam worked as a researcher at the Institute for Advanced Study at Princeton. From 1951 to 1954 he was a professor at the University of Punjab. Salam taught at Cambridge University from 1954 to 1956 and in 1957 became a professor at Imperial College in London. He has also been the director of the International Centre for Theoretical Physics in Trieste.

Dudley R. Herschbach shared the 1986 Nobel Prize in Chemistry for the contributions of his crossed molecular beam research to the detailed understanding of how chemical reactions take place. Herschbach was born in San Jose, California, USA, on 18 June 1932. He attended Stanford University, where he received a BS in Mathematics in 1954 and an MS in Chemistry in 1955. He next attended Harvard University, where he received an MA in Physics in 1956 and a PhD in Chemical Physics in 1958. Herschbach's advisor for his doctoral research was the noted physical chemist E. Bright Wilson. Wilson (1987) recalls:

> Throughout the work, Herschbach was considered by his colleagues as an innovator in the field, a source of scientific insights, and an enthusiastic and inspirational leader. Highly regarded as a teacher as well as a scientist, Herschbach has influenced many students and colleagues with his sharp insights and broad view of science.

Herschbach taught at the University of California-Berkeley from 1959 to 1963 before becoming a professor at Harvard in 1963. Herschbach regards early support for creative and diligent young scientists as of particular importance:

> In Harvard there is something called a Society of Fellows. It was founded with the idea that the ordinary grind of gaining a PhD is not the right thing for the most creative people. The idea was to have the Society of Fellows where people could — after their Bachelors degree — be independent scholars for three years. It tells these young people who are chosen by some Senior Fellows that interview them, that they are special. I was in the Society of Fellows and it was a marvellous experience. I met with other young people from all different fields, twice a week for lunch. Once a week we had dinner with the Senior Fellows. Any distinguished visitor who was in town always got brought there. The best thing about this sort of thing is the young people interacted with other young people and the Senior Fellows, and they soon realised that they are actually comparable, in terms of intelligence and imagination, to these people. They begin to think why can't they do things that are comparable. It is hard to think of a better thing to do in terms of investing in young people. You have got to encourage people to have the confidence to follow their own ideas. That is crucial in science because lots of times people are not going to have confidence. Often, nature is going to be recalcitrant, and you will have a real battle on your hands before you get somewhere where you can see that maybe this is going to work out after all.

Currently, Herschbach is exploiting the tremendous increase in computing power available to develop new approaches to performing electronic structure calculations.

Richard E. Taylor shared the 1990 Nobel Prize in Physics for a 'breakthrough in our understanding of matter'. By bombarding hydrogen and deuterium with high-energy electrons, he confirmed the existence of quarks, demonstrating that protons and neutrons were not fundamental particles.

Taylor was born in Medicine Hat, Canada, on 2 November 1929. He attended the University of Alberta, where he received a BS in 1950 and an MS in 1952. Taylor received his PhD from Stanford University in 1962. Taylor was a researcher at Boursier Laboratory in France from 1958 to 1961. He did research at Lawrence Berkeley Laboratories from 1961 to 1962. In 1962, he began teaching at Stanford, where he has also been a researcher at the Stanford Linear Accelerator Center (SLAC). Through joint projects at SLAC, Taylor collaborated with his co-laureates at the Massachusetts Institute of Technology. Waldrop (1990) notes:

> This was a very big project, it involved an awful lot of organisation, and someone, probably the original director, should have got a Nobel Prize for the organisation that built the laboratory that is SLAC. I spent a lot of time in what you have to call organisation, but I didn't think of it as organisation; I thought it was just, well, trying to hold this thing together. I was leading but I was not organised, I was finding people who wanted to get it done, and they were doing the organising bit.

Geoffrey Wilkinson shared the 1973 Nobel Prize in Chemistry for his pioneering work on the chemistry of organometallic 'sandwich' compounds, including the preparation and the elucidation of the structure of ferrocene.

Wilkinson was born in Todmoren, England, on 14 July 1921. He attended the University of London, where he received his BSc in 1941 and his PhD in 1946. Wilkinson was a Scientific Officer at the National Research Council of Canada from 1943 to 1946, working on a wartime atomic energy project. He was a researcher from 1946 to 1950 at the Lawrence Radiation Laboratory at the University of California-Berkeley. While a research associate at the Massachusetts Institute of Technology, Wilkinson shifted fields from nuclear chemistry to inorganic chemistry. Wilkinson taught at Harvard from 1951 to 1955 before finally becoming a professor at the University of London in 1956.

Wilkinson has strong views, many of which he expressed in a forthright way to me. On the need for support for research he said:

> You can't do great research without good support — financial, organisational and also the input of students.

He has a very individual orientation to his work, relying on himself as the main source of ideas and their development:

> I am not interested in Science in general. I find most of chemistry either too boring or complicated for my liking. What I like to do is to work in areas where I don't have to do any literature surveys. My ideal paper has either no references at all or the references are all to myself. I have, however, only achieved this maybe once or twice.

Herbert A. Hauptman shared the 1985 Nobel Prize in Chemistry for his development of direct methods for the determination of three-dimensional crystal structures of molecules.

Hauptman was born in the Bronx, New York, USA, on 14 February 1917. He received his BS from the City College of New York in 1937, his MA from Columbia University in 1939 and his PhD from the University of Maryland in 1955. Hauptman was a statistician for the US Census Bureau from 1940 to 1942. He served in the US Air Force from 1942 to 1943 and from 1946 to 1947. From 1947 to 1970, Hauptman was a researcher at the United States Naval Research Laboratory, where he collaborated with his co-laureate Jerome Karle. In 1970, he became an administrator at the Medical Foundation of Buffalo, New York.

Hauptman was central to the development of direct methods for the determination of three-dimensional crystal structures of molecules. Crystal structure analysis is so successful because it is unique in providing an unambiguous and complete three-dimensional representation of the atoms in a crystal. Other chemical and physical methods of structure determination merely provide relationships from which the number and nature of atoms bonded to each atom present (molecular topology) can be found or for simple molecules some quantitative information from which geometrical details can be deduced. No other method can give the entire detailed picture that X-ray and neutron diffraction can produce.

The Nobel Prize award in 1985 for H. Hauptman and J. Karle has had a tremendous effect on the revolution of single-crystal X-ray diffraction studies in chemistry and biology. The development of computers from the 1950s to the present day has enabled the evolution of computer programs for the solution and refinement of crystal structures. The development of 'direct methods' (at the heart of which lies the phase problem) by Hauptman and Karle in combination with the computer programs on more powerful computers has led to an exponential increase in the number of published crystal structures in the chemical literature. It is pertinent to note that the basic four-circle diffractometer has changed little over the past thirty years so that equipment has had little effect on this dramatic increase, which has been mainly due to the evolution of computers and programs.

Baruj Benacerraf shared the 1980 Nobel Prize in Medicine or Physiology for contributions to the understanding of genetically determined cell-surface structures that regulate immunological reactions. In particular, he determined that genes in the major histocompatibility complex control the cell interactions responsible for human immune response.

Benacerraf was born in Caracas, Venezuela, on 29 October 1920. He attended the Lycée Janson in France, receiving his Baccalaureate in 1940. In 1942 he received his BS from Columbia University and in 1945 he received an MD from the Medical College of Virginia. Benacerraf was a physician at Queens General Hospital in New York from 1945 to 1946. He served in the US Army from 1946 to 1948 and then returned to Columbia University, where he was a researcher from 1948 to 1950. From 1950 to 1956, he was an administrator at the Centre National de Recherche Scientifique, France. Benacerraf returned to the US and was a professor at New York University from 1956 to 1968. (It was during this period that he concentrated his research on the cells involved in the immune responses, the body's defence system against foreign substances.) He spent two years as an administrator at the National Institutes of Health in Bethesda, Maryland, from 1968 to 1970. In 1970, he became a professor and administrator at Harvard University, where he also became the president of the Dana-Farber Cancer Institute.

Benacerraf's bouts of asthma as a child led to his interest in the mechanism of immune hypersensitivity, an abnormal response of the body to foreign agents. Wilson (1987) notes:

> Benacerraf was unable to establish his own laboratory and thus advance his scientific career in France. He believed that his status as a foreign scientist was impeding his progress in the European scientific community.

He described how he became interested in research into immunity:

> I started doing some experiments when I was in medical school because I was interested in it and the process of finding things that are not known. I decided that is what I wanted to do and I was attracted to immunology as a field that I wanted to get into. This was primarily because I had asthma as a child so it was an area that interested me. I wanted to learn more about the diseases concerning hypersensitivity so I decided to get into training in that field and to ask questions about the mechanism of hypersensitivity and that's when I began. Rapidly I found it was not difficult to find answers to these problems, but the problems as I had placed them were minor compared to the larger problem on the field which had to do with immunity. What other molecule? What other gene? As time went on and my career evolved to a point where I had a laboratory of my own in New York University in the late 1950s. By that time I was both trained and mature enough to begin to ask questions that are much more serious. I was no longer asking questions about the hypersensitive mechanism of disease which I contributed to in a variety of ways and I was asking more fundamental questions: such as 'what is meant by immunity?' and 'what is meant by recognition?' and 'how is it controlled?' By that time I was lucky, because in my opinion discoveries are always made accidentally. You ask a question, you like to understand something and you design an experiment that you are going to do. During the course of the observations that you make serendipity is very important because something happens that will attract your attention and will orient the nature of the research in a somewhat different direction or at least a more realistic one. That happens to me many times and you take advantage of your past experience and your past observations to build upon it.

Heinrich Rohrer shared the 1986 Nobel Prize in Physics for his design of the scanning tunnelling electron microscope, which has found applications in semiconductor physics, atomic structures of biological macromolecules and low-temperature physics.

Rohrer was born in Buchs, Switzerland, on 6 June 1933. He attended the Swiss Federal Institute of Technology, where he received his Diploma in 1955 and his PhD in 1960. Rohrer was a researcher at the Swiss Institute of Technology from 1960 to 1961. After a few years as a researcher at Rutgers University in New Jersey, from 1961 to 1963, he returned to Switzerland, becoming a researcher at IBM Switzerland in 1963. One of his colleagues at IBM was Gerd Binnig, his co-laureate.

He told me about the importance of being able to think freely, without being constrained by conventional methods and frameworks. Yet he is aware of an irony that exists, in which to be able to think freely, we have to know existing science. He explains:

> Perhaps the scientific method constrains us and we should be freer to think in a freer framework. But I think that's unavoidable because you have to learn first what actually exists. Of course if you take that which exists as the full truth, then when the crucial moment comes, what you have learned, though you have to take it as the truth, yet not everything of it is the full truth. Maybe we should learn more and more that under what circumstances this is how it should be. That is why we use experiments and also use a theoretical framework. An experiment only makes sense when you also give the circumstances under which you have done the experiment. Under these conditions very often something is established. Newtonian mechanics explained much of the world we knew, but the known world is now larger, so classical mechanics, though inadequate, is not in principle wrong. If you think classical mechanics is wrong because quantum mechanics is different, then I think one makes a mistake; one should look at classical mechanics as a special case of quantum mechanics. In fact, if you think about it, maybe quantum mechanics might in the future prove to be a special case of something else!
>
> Quantum mechanics might be a special case of something which would allow us to approach complexity, and all complex systems such as the biological system, in a more natural way, in a more effective way. But we simply have to be aware that quantum mechanics is not the end of wisdom, let's put it that way.

Antony Hewish shared the 1974 Nobel Prize in Physics for his discovery of pulsars, compact radio sources that emit regular pulses.

Hewish was born in Fowey England on 11 May 1924. He attended Cambridge University, where he received his BA in 1948, his MA in 1950 and his PhD in 1952. In 1952, Hewish became a professor at Cambridge University. Findlay (1974) notes:

> British astronomy has not been without its critics over the past years, and in some branches of the science it is possible to criticize the lack of a sensible long-term policy. But in radio astronomy there has clearly been a policy. British radio astronomy has been supported in the two centres of excellent work, at Cambridge and at Manchester. This has been a concentration of efforts and funds; the small but good group at the Royal Radar Establishment has been allowed to lapse. Funds for new instruments have, up to now, alternated between the Jodrell Bank (Manchester) and Cambridge groups ... Both observatories are associated with universities which supply excellent graduate students in radio astronomy.

When describing his early scientific experiences, Hewish was unassuming:

I didn't have any expectation about being a brilliant scientist or anything like that. I got myself a first class degree but that doesn't mean much. I had an interrupted academic career. I had three years war service, I had to come back to Cambridge to finish off my degree so I worked very hard when I got back and got myself a first class degree. But I have never regarded myself as particularly clever. I was always interested in scientific things and so forth but it was in about my second year as a research student that I had this idea about radio waves propagating through the atmoionosphere. It was a theoretical thing. I didn't regard myself as a theorist. In fact I never had done. I regard myself as somebody who makes observations more than a theorist. But this was a good theoretical idea which had not been thought of by the theoreticians. And it impressed Jack Radcliffe who was then head of what was called radio physics in the Cavendish and he took an enormous interest in this and of course that gave me a good boost. I had done a couple of papers and that was when I realised that I had actually done something. ...I was thinking about what you can learn from the way radio waves propagate through the atmosphere as a kind of spin-off from radio astronomy looking at radio waves from outer space, and as they come through the atmosphere, the atmosphere interrupts them in some sense. It scatters and diffracts them and so on. Eventually you get some information about what is going on up there and I realised that you could use this to interpret some of the atmospheric conditions way above any level that had previously been anticipated. And so I wrote a short theoretical paper about it that contained the germ of an idea that turned out to be a very fruitful one and a mathematical idea.

Baruch S. Blumberg shared the 1976 Nobel Prize in Physiology or Medicine for his 'discoveries concerning mechanisms involved in the origin and spread of infectious diseases'. Specifically, he identified the antigen in blood that is linked to hepatitis B, visualized the virus using electron microscopy and developed a vaccine for hepatitis.

Blumberg was born in New York on 28 July 1925. He studied physics and mathematics at Union College in New York, receiving his BS in 1946. He received an MD from Columbia University in 1951, then studied biophysical problems in chemistry at Oxford University, earning his PhD in 1957. Blumberg was a scientist at the National Institutes of Health in Bethesda, Maryland, from 1957 to 1964. He continued his research at the Institute for Cancer Research in Pennsylvania (now the Fox Chase Cancer Center), in Philadelphia, Pennsylvania in 1964. In 1967 he became a professor of medicine and anthropology at the University of Pennsylvania, teaching courses in medical anthropology. Currently, Blumberg is a researcher at the Fox Chase Cancer Center in Pennsylvania.

While in medical school, Blumberg had worked in a hospital in a mining community in Surinam (then Dutch Guiana) in northern South America. He conducted disease surveys among the indigenous and migrant populations of this largely undeveloped country, and was struck by the large differences in responses to disease and infection, primarily relating to agents associated with filariasis (elephantiasis) and malaria, among the different ethnic groups inhabiting the country. This concern with the question of why some people get sick and others do not — that is, a study of factors related to health as well as those which result in illness — guided much of his later research.

While at Oxford, Blumberg was influenced by the zoological and genetic thinking then prevalent in that institution and in Great Britain.

During this period (of extensive field trips) Blumberg acquired an interest in anthropology, in part because, in many remote places, the only other visitors were anthropologists.

The studies of Blumberg and his colleagues were particularly broad and encompassed many scientific disciplines. Entomological studies showed that the virus may be carried by mosquitoes and bedbugs. There is a curious relation of the virus to the sex of its hosts. Male humans are more likely to become carriers of the virus, and females are more likely to develop antibody to the surface of the antigen after infection. There also appears to be a relationship between the response of parents to hepatitis B infection and the sex of their offspring. There have also been behavioral studies on the social and psychological problems caused by the identification of occult hepatitis carriers who, in some cases, were stigmatized by this biological characteristic.

George H. Hitchings and Gertrude B. Elion shared the 1988 Nobel Prize in Medicine or Physiology for their discoveries in principles of chemotherapy and development of a rational method for drug design. They participated in the design of drugs to selectively combat leukaemia, malaria, gout and auto-immune disorders.

Hitchings was born in Hoquiam, Washington, USA, on 18 April 1905. He received his BS from the University of Washington in 1927 and his PhD from Harvard University in 1933. Hitchings taught at Harvard from 1933 to 1939 and at Western Reserve University from 1939 to 1942. From 1942 to 1975, he was a researcher at Burroughs-Wellcome Laboratories.

Elion was born in New York on 23 January 1918. She earned her AB in Chemistry from Hunter College in 1937 and her MS from New York University in 1941. She also completed two years' worth of study towards a PhD at Brooklyn Polytechnic Institute (McGrayne, 1993). Elion's professional career included teaching biochemistry to nursing students and working in quality control for a supermarket chain. McGrayne (1993) notes:

> At first, she learned a good deal about instrumentation. Then, when the work became repetitive, she announced to the boss... 'I have learned whatever you have to teach me, and there's nothing more for me to do. I have to move on.' Persistence kept her going.

Elion was a researcher for the Quaker Maid Company from 1942 to 1943 and for the Johnson and Johnson Company from 1943 to 1944. From 1944 to 1983, she was a researcher at Burroughs-Wellcome. McGrayne (1993) continues:

Burroughs-Wellcome turned out to be a highly unusual company, a British firm owned by a charitable trust. Until 1986 when 25 percent of the company was sold for stock, Burroughs-Wellcome was run solely to benefit the Wellcome Trust, which supports research laboratories and medically related activities like medical museums and libraries. Two American pharmacists, Silas Burroughs and Henry Wellcome, had founded the company in England in 1880. Wellcome wanted the firm to discover drugs to treat serious, incurable diseases. He promised his scientists, 'If you have an idea, I will give you the freedom to develop it.'

Wellcome employed these two prizewinners from the mid 1940s to their recent semi-retirement. One result of this is their citation as co-inventors on 18 patents for purine and pyrimidine metabolites. In the word of a colleague, 'they defined and delineated with unusual ingenuity the pathways of purine and pyrimidine metabolism'. Among the first drugs that emerged from their research were 6-mercaptopurine and thiaguanine, both active against leukaemia, and pyrimethamine and trimethroprim, both used as anti-malarials. More recently Hitchings and Elion developed azathioprine (Imuran), the immunosuppressive drug that has probably been used more than any others to decrease the rate of rejection of transplanted organs. They have also developed allopurinol, the xanthine oxidase inhibitor that is used in the treatment of gout and kidney stones.

Their citation stresses the significance of the anti-metabolite philosophy in the development of the early anti-leukaemia drugs, and later the development of drugs such as acyclovir (an anti-herpes drug). This illustrates the importance placed by the Nobel Committee on the longer term influence of the methods they developed.

3   THE ORGANISATIONAL ABILITY OF THE PRINCIPAL INVESTIGATOR

There is a case to be made that distinguished scientists are people of considerable organisational ability. Of course, a necessary condition is that they have also outstanding ability in science, but this may not be a sufficient condition. There appears to be at least as strong a case to be made for organisational ability as there is for creativity, in relation to success in science. The history of science actually demonstrates this very well, though in fact it has not been highlighted by many commentators.

In discussions with those Nobel laureates who took part in this study, it became apparent that they all had considerable organisational ability. They also had unusual experiences which had perhaps fostered this ability to organise. Benacerraf was born to a business family and found himself running a New York bank while doing post-doctoral research at Harvard. Benacerraf also took great pride in the number of scientists he had helped over the years, many of whom went on to very senior positions in science. Brown had taken charge of a family business when his parents died when he was fourteen years old. Hewish was an officer in the British Army during the last war. Taylor had been involved in the early days setting up the Stanford Linear Accelerator. Hauptman and Blumberg had both served some years as officers in the US Navy.

It would be good to be able to show this organisational ability clearly for all those in this study. However, very few scientists have spoken about this aspect of their work, emphasising rather the purely scientific aspects instead. Even fewer have published anything about their early organisational experience, and much of this information is by way of word of mouth stories. Nevertheless, if personal organisational ability is a key factor in relation to scientific discovery, then there could be substantial implications for the selection of scientists, and for their training and development during their early research.

Three examples are given here of work done by Nobel laureates in this study. The examples are not as complete as one would wish, but a much longer study would be needed with access to the notes of the individuals concerned, and discussions with a wider group of people who were concerned in those projects, in order to do justice to the possible role of organisational ability in these projects. They do illustrate, however, the extraordinary organisational ability of these scientists, in addition to their scientific genius.

Baruch S. Blumberg discovered 'Australia antigen', an antigen associated with viral hepatitis. His work has included determination of the prevalence of the antigen in different geographical regions, studies of the transmission of the antigen, visualisation of the hepatitis virus particles with electron microscopy, and the development of a hepatitis vaccine (Blumberg et al., 1973).

The Australia antigen was discovered in 1963 when 'a precipitin was detected in the blood of a patient with haemophilia which reacted with only a single member of the 24 sera in the test panel; the reacting serum was from an Australian aborigine'. In order 'to determine why a haemophilia patient from New York had developed a precipitin in his serum which reacted with material present in the blood of an Australian aborigine', population studies were conducted to collect sera from normal and diseased patients. It was discovered that the antigen retained its reactivity even in blood samples stored for up to 10 years. This made it possible to include stored blood samples from the Institute for Cancer Research in these studies, samples that had not necessarily been stored with such a study in mind.

Blumberg's research focused in part on isolating and characterising the antigen. Animal studies were conducted to raise antibodies for comparison with those seen in humans whose sera reacted with the Australia antigen. Other studies involved using biochemical techniques such as DEAE-cellulose chromatography, Sephadex column separation, electrophoresis and staining to isolate and characterize the Australia antigen. Eventually, the antigen was visualised by electron microscopy, and nuclei of liver cells with the specificity of the Australian antigen were identified with fluorescent antibodies. These supported the identification of the antigen as a virus.

Another aspect of Blumberg's research was the attempt to link prevalence of the antigen to the spread and development of various diseases. Studies were performed in populations with leukaemia, leprosy and Down's syndrome. Such studies necessitated multicontinent field trips, carefully collected pedigrees and medical information (e.g. transfusion records, measures of liver function, etc.) for each subject, and several years to follow the disease development of the subjects or the genetic transmission of the antigen from parent to child over many generations. Furthermore, for each diseased population that was followed, an appropriate control population needed to be chosen and followed. Large study populations made it possible to analyse the data by breaking them into various subgroups (e.g. Down's syndrome patients in large facilities, small facilities and home settings) and to check the statistical significance of conclusions.

Herbert C. Brown was a pioneer in elucidating the chemistry of boron and its reactions with organic compounds. He developed numerous invaluable techniques in organic synthesis using this chemistry, perhaps most notably anti-Markovnikov additions to alkenes (Brown *et al.*, 1956). Brown's research in organic synthesis was very time and labour intensive. Numerous starting materials for a given synthesis also needed to be synthesised, while most of those that were obtained commercially required some sort of purification. Some solutions had to be prepared freshly each day. Other conditions (e.g. out of contact with air) were required after they were prepared. Due to the nature of the chemical compounds being used, many reactions needed to be done at very low pressure (i.e. under high vacuum) and in the absence of water. Both of these constraints necessitated special equipment and some amount of training in its use.

The syntheses themselves were often multistep processes during which temperature, atmosphere, rate of addition and rate of mixing were controlled. An addition of a reactant might take 45 minutes, subsequent heating of the reaction mixture an hour — time intervals that add up in a complex procedure. Additional time and techniques were required to extract the desired products, calculate yields and apply numerous tests of purity or of chemical identity (gas–liquid chromatography, melting or boiling point, index of refraction, polarimetry, etc.).

The productivity of Brown's research group probably relied heavily on the training of graduate students and technicians. This training included standard organic synthetic techniques, keeping up to date with the organic chemistry literature not only on such techniques but also to identify new ideas and developments. Perhaps most importantly, this training included the meticulous keeping of records useful in duplicating syntheses but also in writing journal communications or articles. The sheer number of communications to the *Journal of the American Chemical Society* from Brown and coworkers is an indication of the success of such intergroup training and communication.

Antony Hewish discovered pulsars while carrying out a survey of radio galaxies utilising interplanetary scintillation. Hewish made his observation using a large radio telescope, with an array of 2048 dipole antennae measuring 470 m by 45 m. Each row of dipole elements was backed by a reflecting screen, and the dipoles were connected by a network of cables. Signals were displayed on multichannel pen recorders (Hewish, 1968).

The scintillation technique that Hewish employed to make measurements of angular sizes 'demanded repeated observations so that every source could be studied at many different solar elongations'. This meant re-surveying the entire range of accessible sky each week and plotting the positions of the measured scintillating radio sources and sky charts in order to distinguish 'genuine' sources from electrical interference. Needless to say, a great deal of data was generated and analysed.

The signals due to pulsars were at first suspected to be electrical interference, especially since the new measurement techniques might show greater sensitivity to such interference than had previous measurements. The process of proving that these signals were due to an actual source beyond the solar system required a team well trained to interpret data, measurements and calculations designed to determine any errors in the instrumentation, painstaking tracking of day-to-day variations in the signals and finally correlation analyses of the data to check against possible mechanisms that could produce such signals as artefacts of a known process. Moreover, the signals in question varied from day to day, and consisted of fast pulses (~ 0.3 s) when they were present. Thus, the importance of accurate recording of data from the radio telescope cannot be overstated. Unlike a high-speed particle physics experiment, which also depends on intricate equipment being in good order, a radio astronomy observation cannot be made equally well at any time the equipment and technicians are ready. Rather, the astronomers are a captive audience to fleeting phenomena which may appear erratically. Hence, to draw meaningful quantitative conclusions, constant observation over a year or longer may be required.

Not unlike linear accelerators, large observatories often host many researches with different interests and different observational goals. They may be interested in phenomena at different frequencies, in different regions of the sky. To balance such demands, not only must equipment maintenance and standardisation be excellent, but rational plans must be developed to make many of the desired measurements simultaneously. Accurate records must be kept of when and how each data recording is generated, and large amounts of data must be scrutinised to locate the bits that are useful to each investigator.

Let us examine now in more detail the organisational dimension of Blumberg's research. The following work can be discerned in his papers:

(a) Samples of blood were collected from patients and others. This required the obtaining of the appropriate permissions, collaboration with physicians and hospitals, and complex record-keeping.

(b) Geographical studies required field trips to four continents. This required not only funding but also legwork to take blood samples, collect and maintain adequate patient records, perform immunodiffusion tests (for the presence of antibodies to the antigen in the collected blood samples) and perform statistical analyses of the data.

(c) Further data on the antigen in populations with Down's syndrome and leprosy were obtained from other institutions, an example of collaboration and information sharing (or data collection sharing) between institutions.

(d) Studies of the genetic transmission of the antigen relied on field trips, blood sampling, the taking of pedigrees and the sampling of blood from the offspring of subjects. To follow the subjects over two or three generations required good record-keeping and follow-up over several years.

(e) Biochemical testing of viruses and blood products requires specialised equipment and trained technicians to use this equipment, in addition to special treatment and disposal of potentially biohazardous materials. Regulations for biohazards have become increasingly complex.

(f) Animal studies require large populations of test and control animals, which must be cared for in specialised facilities by trained technicians. Regulations dealing with proper treatment and disposal of experimental animals have also become increasingly complex.

It is difficult to exaggerate the importance of organisation in Blumberg's research. Large numbers of scientists had to be selected, trained, managed, motivated and co-ordinated. Blood samples had to be taken, stored, analysed, recorded and summarised. In the middle of this array of activity someone had to keep an overview of the whole project and its aims, and all people had to be able to detect both important and unimportant findings.

It seems clear that Blumberg must have had considerable organisational ability, in order to keep control of the multiple activities described in relation to this project. His capacity to select and motivate colleagues and his infectious enthusiasm must have been extensive. In addition, his ability to remain free of external organisational control, yet use extensive organisational resources, must have been extraordinary, given the originally unknown outcomes of this large and far-reaching project.

The organisational and leadership characteristics of eminent scientists have been ignored in spite of pervasive evidence that organisation plays a key role in discovery. All 166 Nobel laureates in the sciences work in organisations. All these organisations are well-resourced and highly developed.

4   THE RESOURCES OF THOSE ORGANISATIONS IN WHICH THESE SCIENTISTS MADE THEIR DISCOVERIES

It is the general hypothesis of this study that discovery is more likely to occur when dedicated scientists (a) work in well-resourced laboratories and (b) are themselves good organisers. The first part of this hypothesis is supported in that the Nobel laureates in this study all worked in well-resourced laboratories. How well resourced is shown by Table 5.

We can see from Table 5 that in terms of budget, library resources, technical support and the availability of exceptional colleagues, these laboratories are organisationally very rich indeed. The ability to call on extensive resources such as these to the service of some scientific project is a clear example of organisational support. Of course good arguments will have to be made by the principal investigator, to justify these resources, to very talented scientists who can probably think of many other ways to use them. Nevertheless, they are there. The advantage, too, that Herschbach in Harvard, for example, had to drop in on E. Bright Wilson, and in Berkeley, Polanyi, and discuss a difficult problem, is truly very great. Comparisons with other universities, institutes and commercial laboratories might be an odious project. We are aware, in any case, that most such institutions world-wide have very small amounts of discretionary funds for research. Only a few (perhaps in the hundreds) have resources comparable to those described in Table 5.*

Crane (1965) showed a remarkably clear organisational effect on discovery. In her study of 97 major and minor universities in the United States, publication of a major work took place much sooner in a major university, as shown in Table 6. Her study also showed that scientific productivity was significantly higher in the top 12 universities (45%) compared to all other universities (18%). The conclusion of this study is clearly that graduates at major universities were more likely to be highly productive than those from minor universities. However, the reason for this is attributed in Crane's conclusions, not so much to organisational support, but to a selection effect; major universities can select the best and brightest students. Interestingly, though Crane details many organisational effects, she does not conclude that organisational factors are of key importance. Nevertheless, the major universities in the study were acknowledged to select the best students, hire the best academics and provide the best research support. These amount in effect to organisational effects of some importance.

---

*This table is based on the institutions where the sixteen Nobel laureates did their formative research. There are twelve institutions in the table because some of the laureates did their research in the same institutions.

Table 5 Organisational resources in Nobel laureates' institutions

Resources	Cambridge (Cavendish Laboratory)	Dana-Farber	SLAC	IBM Zurich	Imperial College London	Fox Chase Cancer Center	Hauptmann Woodward Medical Center	Harvard Chemistry Department	CERN	Burroughs Wellcome	Purdue University	ETH Zurich
Annual budget in million US$[a]	18.33	88	140	40	4.83	39	2.7	12	784.9	326	9.4	51.88
Annual budget of parent	439.92	6.4	US Department of Energy $17 billion	4500	244.4	115	N/A	1.4 billion	—	—	386	820
Number of researchers in laboratory	460	1000	200 staff 1700 outside users	110		54	26	20	935	742	45	220
Number of research assistants			60 300 in outside group	45	N/A	N/A	5	330	169	N/A	40	176
Number of technicians	150	359	400	15	26		4	10	1065	70	40	88
Number of very distinguished scientists	12	1	8:2 Nobel laureates, 6 National Academy of Science	10	3	1 Nobel laureate 5 National Academy of Science	1	4	5	2	1	6
Books in parent or associated library	5 000 000	12.6 million	6.1 million	4.9 million	650 000	12.6 million	7 million	12.6 million	N/A	UNC 4.4 DUKE 6.0 NSCU 2.4	2.14 million	5 million
Books in own library	12 000	6000	20 000	7000	22 000	22 000	2000	53 000	50 000	14 000	40 000 chemistry	—

[a]All figures have been converted to US dollars at Spring 1996.

Table 6   Publication of first major work by current academic affiliation[a]

	Current academic affiliation		
	Major university	High minor university	Low minor university
Publication of first major work			
Number of years after PhD			
0–5	72	56	43
6–10	22	35	19
Over 10 years	6	9	33
No information	0	0	5
Total	100	100	100
(N)	(54)	(23)	(21)
$\chi^2 = 14.16$, 4 d.f., $p < 0.01$			

[a]Includes only those with major publications.

Andrews (1967) was one of the few creativity researchers who felt that all discovery might not lie entirely within the power of the scientist. In his study of the laboratory environment, he measured creativity (on the remote associations test) and related these results to creative output and to laboratory environment. According to Andrews (1967, p. 82):

> ...creative ability, as we measured it, did not relate to any measure of performance for any group of our scientists. The reason, however, was because some scientists were in situations where creative ability seemed to hurt their performance.

The organisational richness described in Table 5 is very favourable to the dedicated scientist. If we look at the effects of each on research, we can understand their impact. Distinguished colleagues are a most important resource for:

(a) the discussion of ideas,
(b) project design,
(c) encouragement,
(d) networking with other scientists in related areas,
(e) reputation in order to release funding.

Zuckermann has shown that the existence of distinguished colleagues in the laboratory is a powerful stimulus to exceptional endeavour. According to Zuckermann, the particular group a young researcher joins is of immense importance to his or her development.

Zuckermann (1977) found a high incidence of Nobel laureates had carried out research at an early stage in their career, with those who were already

Nobel laureates, or who were about to be. She gives three reasons for this being a significant factor in their own success. Firstly, the Nobel laureates they studied under had very demanding scientific standards. Secondly, they had good styles of work which the younger scientist absorbed. And thirdly, they developed their already considerable talents and grew in confidence from their interaction with these scientists.

Budget is important because it permits things to happen: the provision of research assistants, equipment, time, materials and conference attendance, for example. Library resources are important to access a wide variety and depth of previous research. Perhaps, though, the existence of this resource on site is less important than it was due to the development of CD ROM databases and the Internet, which allows remote searches in well-resourced libraries to take place. The speed of the inter-library loan system makes this a good alternative system.

Research assistants allow the extension of one's own mind and speculation, by the work and ideas of other scientists, to pursue avenues that might otherwise be neglected. The Internet makes collaboration with colleagues — even the most eminent — at least theoretically possible. True, dedicated scientists in distant places may be less enthusiastic about approaches from colleagues not involved in their local research. Nevertheless, nothing but an internal psychological barrier prevents scientists involved in related research from bouncing ideas off even the most eminent of scientists. If these ideas prove to be interesting, they can be assured of fast and detailed responses.

Our discoverer-scientist must be endowed also with clarity of vision in their scientific field, and dedication and persistence in pursuit of their goals, coupled with exceptional skill in organising, leading and creating enthusiasm. This hypothesis is more difficult to prove. Certainly we can look at the success of their experimentation and their obvious discovery, and say *post hoc* that they have these abilities. It would, however, be even more useful if we could identify these capacities at the point of selection of a young scientist. Nevertheless, interesting selection options do exist. These are discussed in Chapter 6.

The next chapters, which treat method, freedom and chance, explore these key factors related to discovery from the point of view of the potential role of organisation in relation to them.

Chapter 5

Organisational Aspects of Freedom and Chance in Relation to Discovery

1 FREEDOM AND DISCOVERY

Freedom is a difficult concept from the organisational viewpoint. To managers and to CEOs, the word 'freedom' suggests a license to spend money on expensive staff and equipment, without any necessary responsibility for the effective use of resources. It suggests an absence of responsibility and of the appropriate control and supervision.

To the creative person, however, freedom is not an option, but essential as the air we breathe. Control and supervision are, to them, synonymous with confinement, restraint, dullness and the status quo. Of course, no one can be entirely free. No scientist is given unlimited funds or has unlimited time. However, attempts by the organisation to place projects under strict control and supervision may place the dead hand of control on the work of a creative and dedicated scientist, and are likely to destroy that person's creativity and energy.

The scientific research laboratory which is geared towards discovery and to the solution of novel problems is a very special organisational situation, which is quite different from the traditional organisation. If it is a successful or promising group, it is comprised of a group of highly trained and motivated people and has a principal investigator who is a creative and imaginative person, with the ability to range across disciplinary boundaries. The danger is that organisational controls may interfere with his or her capacity to think and experiment freely. This could result in the person leaving the project or experiencing a diminution of creative ideas and energy (and its related hard work). Freedom in thinking suggests the ability to move outside the narrow

Table 7 Nobel laureates' (rank ordered, $n = 14$) responses on the 'freedom' questionnaire

No.	Question	Mean	Standard error of mean
Scale: 1–4 importance			
9	Freedom of thought	4.00	0.0
1	Being able to choose what I work on	3.92	0.08
8	Independence of thought	3.92	0.08
3	Freedom to use my own judgement	3.83	0.11
2	Free to choose my own problems	3.73	0.14
6	Working to a defined research plan	2.67	0.22
5	Pressure from being supervised	2.18	0.38
4	Working as part of a team	2.17	0.30
7	Pressure from peers	1.83	0.21
Scale: 1–4 agree, disagree			
13	My work gives me unexpected rewards	3.77	0.12
14	Positive climate of innovation in lab	3.58	0.15
17	Scope for playfulness in my work	3.01	0.28
16	Stimulating physical ambience in lab	3.00	0.28
18	Security of employment	2.62	0.35
10	Frameworks of existing science are best guesses	2.45	0.31
12	I have limited freedom in my research	2.00	0.28
11	Frameworks of existing science are incontrovertible descriptions	1.91	0.21
15	I work best under pressure of evaluation	1.77	0.20

confines of the stated problem. This is important because it may be incorrectly posed, and may even appear to detach itself from the research project. However, a creative and dedicated mind may well be in the process of redefining our understanding of the problem in some fundamental way. For example, the creative scientist may notice analogies in other fields which suggest solutions in the present one. For this to happen, he/she must be free to range widely in many areas, so that instinctual ideas can be followed.

Organisational control and supervision, and logical project design and reporting, can damage the very fruitfulness of the project, which presumably needs to be protected. The views of the present sample of eminent scientists would be useful to examine at this point. Table 7 gives the results of the questionnaire completed by the sample of Nobel laureates in this study.

Table 7 gives the participants mean responses on two questionnaires related to freedom. The first six questions are rated between 3 and 4 on the four-point scale, indicating their view of these as all extremely important. These include freedom of thought, choice of work, independence of thought, freedom of judgement, freedom to select problems, and a positive climate in the lab.

These results show that the respondents agreed strongly that their work gives them unexpected rewards, that there is a positive climate of innovation in their lab and that there is scope for playfulness in their work. However, they strongly disagreed that the frameworks of existing science are incontrovertible descriptions, or that they have limited freedom in their research, or that they work best under the pressure of evaluation. The results show that they attach maximum possible (near to 4 on a four-point scale) importance to those aspects of this questionnaire relating to their own freedom of thought and behaviour, including their ability to choose their own work. This is in sharp contrast with their responses on the questions relating to the importance of supervision and planning. The likelihood of discovery occurring in a research laboratory is seen by our Nobel laureates as strongly related to the degree to which freedom of thought and independence of action is part of the culture of the laboratory. According to Herschbach:

> A good scientist wants to do the best he/she can. Anything that limits the freedom to do that diminishes the chance that significant results will be achieved. Likewise vital, is freedom to learn what others are finding out.

And according to Richard Ernst:

> I think it helped me that I was allowed great freedom in my research by my supervisor who influenced me greatly. Resources were also provided to allow me the freedom to research and develop my ideas.

They did not see pressure from a supervisor, or working as part of a team, or working to a defined plan as of importance in their work. Herchsbach comments on this question:

> But (I felt) far less so than the pressure from myself that stems from a love of science, and a yearning to make a significant contribution.

In other words, his own internal pressures and motivations were far more important than any external pressure.

Freedom of thought

Most of the scientists in this study had chosen their doctoral projects themselves, while some had been given a project by their supervisor. In this latter case their respect for their supervisor, and for the importance of the general area of the problem, was such that they had no difficulty incorporating it into their way of thinking. In fact, the nature of the project changed under their study to become essentially different in character, as it proceeded to resolve the particular problem.

In either case, their absolute control over the thinking and experimentation in relation to the problem was unquestioned, though they were expected to share all results with the supervisor and other colleagues who were involved. It was clear when speaking to each of these people that they were unusually unconcerned about the opinions and views (however strongly held) of other people, even, or perhaps particularly, those in important authority positions.

For example, when he was a young researcher, Wilkinson had no difficulty when reading a textbook in deciding that the structure given for ferrocene was wrong, despite the fact that it was the received wisdom of the time.

This strong independence of thought, and the view of existing frameworks as being rather more best guesses than precise incontrovertible descriptions, is a very important aspect of the personality of the scientist. Bargar and Duncan (1982, p. 12), in a study of creative endeavour in doctoral research, concluded that:

> Science can excite the mind best when the scientist is free to play with ideas and create new forms that are intrinsically meaningful and 'beautiful' to him; in other words when he can engage in the creation of scientific thought and research that draws upon the depths of his experience, values and commitments as a human being as well as upon his knowledge and skill. Once created, scientific concepts can be subjected to empirical test, but the scientist must first be free to be motivated and to create original thought forms. Under these conditions, his mind may move from intuitive imagery to logical analysis, to empirical test, and back again in a natural productive cycle. This cannot happen when science is viewed solely as an enterprise in logic or when authority over ideas is vested in the 'great scientists' and in an already extant body of knowledge.

In a beautifully frank admission of his failure to discover relativity theory, Hadamard (1988) tells us:

> To think that this Kirchhoff line did not have a physical significance—that was too bold a leap for me. Like all mathematicians I admired the vast and ever expanding body of work that was being produced by physicists; this admiration mingled with respect imposed by my own incompetence. I had not yet clearly understood that one should be able on occasion be able to fail to show respect to physics.

If scientists who are daunted by the existing structures of science become the dominant group in research, it would seem unlikely that new and important insights will be achieved. Yet, of course, every scientist must be familiar with much of the historical and existing body of related scientific knowledge. This reveals a paradox, which it is difficult to resolve. Some scientists, perhaps most, will have so much respect for progress to date that they may always be daunted by the existing body of knowledge, and accept existing frameworks without criticism. Few will be able to see beyond this and to imagine that which does not yet exist. All of this suggests strong organisational implications for the selection, the training, the supervision, and the group structures, for both kinds of scientist.

Co-ordination in research

Is it possible to successfully co-ordinate a complex investigation, if every research scientist is free to pursue his or her own particular interest? At a time when scientific research is so expensive, scientific freedom is often seen as a recipe for time-wasting disorganisation. Consequently, the necessity to introduce control, organisation and co-ordination is seen as of paramount importance to the success of a research project. An irony emerges here. Those laboratories that are (in the industrial sense) most organised, controlled and focused on the production of a desired commercial or military project, in most cases depend on the university laboratories to produce something new in science!

In university laboratories, where freedom is valued highly, there is a very different kind of organisation. University laboratories are typically organised to facilitate the work of large numbers of doctoral people carrying out their individual research projects. The motivation comes from the individuals, and the laboratory provides (as much as it can) the necessary conditions. Questions as to whether particular projects will be economically or socially useful are usually not considered.

However, the distinction between university-based laboratories and commercial industry-based ones is no longer clear-cut. Some commercial laboratories appear to be organised on similar lines to those in universities and, increasingly, some university laboratories are organised on a commercial basis. George Hitchings describes his early years at Burroughs Wellcome as being extraordinarily free. He was asked to explore the possibility of developing cancer-treating drugs. Hitchings' doctoral work had been involved in research into the nature of adenosine triphosphate. He was then (in 1942) the sole member of the Biochemistry Department. He decided to go back to the basics and examine the nature of DNA. According to Hitchings (1989):

> I saw the opportunity to explore nucleic acid biosynthesis in a new and revealing way by employing synthetic analogues of purine and pyramidine bases in a system utilising these heterocyclic compounds for biosynthesis.

The idea was to try to discover cell growth inhibitory compounds of use in a variety of diseases. By 1947, Hitchings' group, which now included Elvira Falco and Gertrude Elion, had synthesised a number of compounds which appeared to show signs of selective inhibition. These included 2,6-diamino-purine and 6-mercaptopurine, which were sent for trial at the Sloan Kettering Cancer Institute, with strongly positive results. Some rapid remissions in leukaemia took place, much to the delight of the research group. The success of this early research gave Hitchings, Elion, Falco and their colleagues an early reward in line with their values, and a substantial feeling that in science it is really possible to do useful things. Elion tells us:

> If you really want to know what I think about the secret of research, it is to have that freedom, to follow where the research leads you, and not to be told that you are a chemist and you have no business worrying about the metabolic aspects. I see it happening around in other companies, people are kept in their little niche and they really don't develop.

Notable in the Hitchings/Elion experience is the length of time spent (about five years) and permitted by the laboratory before anything useful emerged, and the absolute freedom which Hitchings was given. It was also commercially very fruitful.

This security of tenure, and for planning the research, is an important organisational dimension to freedom. Security allows people to be free. Fear and anxiety have a role in freedom because not everyone is willing to be truly free in their thoughts. The organisation and the support of one's colleagues, can greatly help the individual researcher, who must somehow develop the courage to constantly think in his or her own direction. In other words, he/she must not be unduly influenced by those who dismiss or ridicule new ideas as being 'half-baked' notions. This organisational support is vital because half-baked ideas with some creative content, can change the direction of research in a way which fully developed ideas of no new content, will certainly not.

2 CHANCE AND DISCOVERY

Chance is widely perceived by the general public and among scientists as being of considerable importance in scientific progress. The literature abounds with examples of chance factors influencing (if not causing) discoveries. Fleming's discovery of penicillin, Pasteur's development of the cholera vaccine and Minkowski's discovery that diabetes arises from a disorder of the pancreas are all familiar examples of discoveries 'arising from' chance.

Ernst Mach in his inaugural professorial address, in 1895, spoke about 'the part played by accident in invention and discovery'. He listed a number of discoveries which appear to have arisen from accidental happenings. He referred, for example, to the story of a boiling tea-kettle lifting the lid repeatedly, which gave James Watt the idea for the steam engine, and Schoenbein's discovery of ozone by smelling something different in the air around electric sparks. Interestingly, his address makes a different point much more strongly. In all his examples the part played by careful observation, a prepared mind and analogous thinking demonstrate very clearly the way by which the trained and enthusiastic scientist capitalises on accident or chance. Accidental or chance phenomena occur frequently, and are probably in themselves unimportant. Chance phenomena may be important not in themselves, but only in that they stimulate thinking. Only in some cases, and with some scientists, do they suggest new insights.

In attributing discovery to chance, we diminish it and locate it in some magical area, beyond our capacity to influence. We effectively remove from human influence the surrounding environment of science, and abrogate our own ownership and responsibility for it. If we subscribe to Edison's view that invention is 99% perspiration and 1% inspiration, then a reliance on chance downgrades perspiration and upgrades inspiration. It is possible that this way of thinking has led to a lack of interest in the organisation of research because, if chance is so important, then organisation could have very little influence on discovery. This view is probably to the detriment of discovery, since the record of most scientific discovery is more a record of good organisation than it is of chance. This good organisation concerns the team, the experiments needed, the support systems and the wider administrative system, and sets the scene for the well-prepared scientist to capitalise on chance opportunities.

In an article that explores the details of these three discoveries, Root-Bernstein (1988) questions the decisive role of chance in them. He points out that in the details of the events leading up to these discoveries (as distinct from shorthand versions) there is evidence of a chance factor occurring. There is, however, much more evidence of a trained mind observing these happenings, and trained technicians in a well-organised and prepared laboratory being ready to benefit from any occurrence (accidental or otherwise) in relation to the study:

> Virtually every so-called chance discovery that has been re-examined in the light of additional historical evidence, has had to be revised in the manner of the Pasteur, Minkowski and Fleming stories. Again and again the record reveals that discovery is not a fluke, but the inevitable if unforeseen consequence of a rational and carefully planned line of inquiry initiated by a scientist. It follows that contrary to philosophical orthodoxy, the tests of an incorrect hypothesis often result in surprises that lead to discovery, and that discoverers are not just beneficiaries of fate.

Sutton (1986) takes a similar view that too much discovery has been attributed to chance. She cites the case of Becquerel whose discovery of radioactivity is widely attributed to chance. The salts of uranium which Becquerel used were luminescent and glowed brightly after exposure to the sun. Becquerel knew that his photographic plates darkened when exposed to the luminescent salts. One day, 'by chance', he decided to develop the plates which had been exposed to the uranium, even though the salts were not luminescent. He discovered the plates had images on them created by the salts. He had expected to find only 'feeble images' but found strong ones. This process has been attributed to chance. However, it seems much more likely that this was the normal work of a curious scientist, following up a possible lead.

For the present study, the author administered a questionnaire on chance to the sixteen Nobel laureates, which asked them to rate its importance on a four-point scale, with 4 meaning 'very important'. The author also attempted to investigate whether or not a distinction existed between cognitive chance and magical chance by means of the questionnaire. Cognitive chance was defined as 'the intersection of opportunity with preparedness', while magical chance was defined as 'some non-explainable haphazard occurrence over which you have no control, such as your birth position in your family or being born with a high IQ'.

Table 8 Results of the questionnaire study on chance

No. Question	Mean response ($n = 12$)	Standard error of mean
1 Importance of 'magical' chance factors in your life generally?	3.46	0.14
2 Importance of 'magical' chance factors in relation to your creative scientific discoveries?	3.17	0.24
3 Importance of 'cognitive' chance factors in your life generally?	3.0	0.30
4 Importance of 'cognitive' chance factors in relation to your creative scientific discoveries?	3.17	0.27

The results given in Table 8 show that our Nobel laureates considered chance 'important' at the level of 3 on the four-point scale, but not very important. Also it is clear from these results that they do not distinguish between cognitive and magical chance (in this terminology), which would indicate that they consider both types of chance of equal importance. However, in their written responses in relation to these questions, differing views emerged. Many laureates felt that in some very general sense chance factors were at work in their lives. They mention the role of chance in being born in a certain country, or a city, or in comfortable circumstances. However, they attached less importance in these written responses to the role of chance directly in relation to their discoveries. Brown tells us:

My discoveries are largely the result of systematic research, and the ability to recognise the importance of unexpected results.

And Elion says something rather similar:

The ability to recognise opportunities when they arose, guided my research quite often, especially in the early years.

In responding to question 1, in the 'Chance' questionnaire, Herschbach felt that the question could be interpreted in two quite different ways. He clarifies the role of chance in his life in the following way:

Obviously, if as probability would have it, I had been born as a Chinese peasant, my life would have been very different. So again, I would have to say that 'non-explainable haphazard occurrences over which I have no control' was 'very important'. Yet, a more meaningful answer requires normalising to 'typical trajectories' of similar people so then my answer becomes 'unimportant'.

Blumberg makes the following point in relation to the chance questions when he says:

A prepared mind is necessary as well as planned experiments and adequate theories, but are not sufficient for discovery.

Hannan, Roy and Christman (1988) cite Herbert Brown as attributing his interest in the borons to a gift of a book on the chemistry of borons from his then fiancée. They interpret this as a chance factor. However, this supports a different phenomenon from chance; it supports the influence that significant others can have on a scientist's motivation. This in turn is related to group dynamics, a matter that can be strongly influenced by the organisation in which the research takes place.

Chance can be viewed in many ways, as we have seen in Herschbach's example. Two quite different views are easily distinguishable. The first view of chance is the notion of random chance favouring certain individuals; the other is that chance is the intersection of opportunity with preparedness. Pasteur puts it: 'In fields of observation chance favours only the prepared mind.' Medawar (1985) in a very similar way says:

...it would be injudicious to credit to luck, the consequences of a conscious preparedness of mind.

Indeed, it would be difficult to identify the luck (in the magical sense), if it really exists, of one individual compared to another. However, the second definition of chance, relating preparedness with opportunity, is more amenable to exploration. It would seem to follow from this that the person who has been best prepared is more likely to be 'lucky'. Hence, those scientists who have been given the right exposure to good research, good experimental training and good colleagues would seem more likely to see those opportunities that research provides and to benefit from them. Rohrer takes this view strongly when he says:

Chance in the sense of something random, I do not believe in. I think there are a lot of things which simply come along by chance and you do not think about them. I think that is an important part of creativity, that when the unexpected things happen, you notice that this is something new. Many people said that my work with Binnig was a lot of luck. Sure it was luck but I think being lucky doesn't downgrade any achievement, because most people are lucky, and most don't notice that they are.

By its emphasis on chance, much of the literature does tend to downgrade achievement. The pioneering work of Rohrer and Binnig can be attributed much more to curiosity, persistence and hard work than it can to chance, and with greater credibility. Yet chance so fascinates people that they are ready as the Romans were to attribute to Fortuna more than her fair share, at the expense of man's persistence.

Rohrer goes on to diminish chance's influence as follows:

If you are scientifically well prepared and have the openness of mind, and an opportunity arises then you are also prepared to recognise it. If you do recognise it, then other people will say you were lucky. You, within the system, will not see it as luck; you will see it as an opportunity taken when you were prepared to take it.

This argues not for the identification of luck in applicants but for the selection of those who are already very well prepared, with an organisational dedication to their continued development.

Simonton (1988a) attributes scientific creativity to the operation of 'chance permutations' or, in Campbells' (1960) terms, to 'blind variation'. His argument for the existence of random variation in the production of mental elements is useful and explains the role that permutation plays in the juxtaposition of thoughts. However, though he makes the case that these permutations are a pervading fact of mental life, he does not explain how creative selection or analogy-realisation takes place in some people, while the creative solutions remain unnoticed by many others. As Ernst Mach (1943) puts it: 'The facts that inspired many discoveries were seen numbers of times before they were noticed.' Simonton reminds us of a very difficult question: Is what appears to be a chance occurrence, actually accidental? This may seem a paradoxical question, and it is. It could be argued that since discovery always comes as a surprise, it is therefore attributed to chance. Rather, it can be seen as the occurrence of a surprising congruence of events, culminating in a new insight, which seems to the scientist to be chance, since it was unpredicted and unpredictable. The evolutionary process of scientific discovery makes surprise inevitable, but that is not the same as making discovery dependent on chance factors in that process.

There is another way of conceiving chance which is suggested by Campbell and by Simonton. Chance can be seen as occurring all the time, in the random sequencing of stimuli on the mind. Occasionally, however, those chance stimuli, when perceived by the dedicated scientist in relation to the field under study, suggest some new aspect of discovery. Chance may be a kind of background noise in nature, which occasionally leads to helpful insights. Creative solutions are in fact picked up by those minds that are best prepared by education, by value systems and by societal norms to do so. The organisational factors behind such preparation may be invisible or unacknowledged, even by the discoverers, but are key factors nonetheless. Those who have good scientific education, the opportunity to share ideas with advanced thinkers in their area, excellent laboratory and technician support, advanced computing facilities and comprehensive library resources are in a position to capitalise on whatever random permutations present themselves. The interaction between opportunity and preparedness occurs. In contrast, those who are deprived of all or most of the above advantages may well have the same number of 'chance permutations' as mental events, but will never be able to make use of them.

Scientists attribute their own discoveries either to chance or to their own substantial talent, or to both. The attribution of one's success to chance is an extremely modest way of explaining success in science. Typical descriptions by those interviewed in this study of the operation of chance in their creative discoveries include that of Wilkinson:

> The success of a project is largely based upon chance — you do not know what sort of chemistry is going to be found to be of great importance in ten or fifteen years after starting a project.

However, Wilkinson had the dedication and perseverance to develop a field in science, not knowing whether it was going to be important or not, and probably not caring. That it became a field of considerable importance may as much be due to the fact that it was developed as it was to chance.

Hewish makes a similar point and attributes his discovery to chance:

> Luck came into it in that a problem turned up in this area which I could solve. It's like mining. We are all hammering away at the front line and some people hit gold and others don't. . . . I would say that luck has played a large part in my work.

However, these examples also support the likelihood of discovery being related to intelligent activity as much as to chance. What these scientists may be describing is perhaps the surprise nature of their discoveries, rather than the role of chance as their author.

The unanticipated aspect of discovery is perhaps responsible for the feeling that many scientists have, that chance has played an important role in their discoveries. Chance, rather than being some lucky occurrence favouring 'lucky' scientists, may in fact be a subtler but more explainable phenomenon peculiar to the natural world. The occurrence of 'blind variation' as a constant background influence inherent in fundamental science can be an opportunity for the observant and assiduous scientist to make use of these occurrences. Interestingly Hewish adds:

> It should not be difficult to build within a system, facilities which allow luck to operate.

This indicates in Hewish an awareness that the organisation in which science research is embedded can be such as to make discovery more likely.

The history of many discoveries is written and interpreted to suggest that chance played a central role in them. Cannon (1939) describes Galvani observing frogs legs twitch as they touched an iron balustrade. He lays great emphasis on the accident of the legs touching the iron, but what this seems to illustrate better is the preparedness and powers of observation of the scientist, when presented by chance with a natural phenomenon. Coupled with Root-Bernstein's (1988) observations above, this seems to support the view that chance simply provides the opportunities; the scientist must be ready to see meaning where it is presented.

Differences in the organisation of laboratories

In view of the importance our Nobel laureates attach to freedom, it is not surprising that our scientists are somewhat sceptical about the role of their organisation in relation to themselves and their work. Organisations are often seen as essentially controlling and restricting, rather than enabling and facilitating. Indeed, this view is reinforced in much of the organisational literature. Schein (1980), for example, defines the organisation as:

> ...the rational co-ordination of the activities of a number of people for the achievement of some common explicit purpose or goal, through the division of labour and function, and through some hierarchy of authority and responsibility.

This definition is a widely accepted one, and describes accurately enough the organisation of the military, of industry and of most large bureaucracies.

However, scientists might well fear attempts to apply this model of organisation to scientific work, because they see how little it fits the reality of their organisations, however closely it links with others. Most scientists' laboratories are small, and the hierarchy of authority is often absent or even reversed. The key scientist on a project is often (in the leadership sense) at the top of what little hierarchy there may be, and the research director, though obviously more senior, often sees himself or herself as assisting rather than directing the project. Unlike the industrial organisation, the thinking and doing are not separated and at different levels, but unite in individuals involved in the research. Co-ordination takes place around a research problem, not around explicit objectives. Some division of labour takes place, but will fluctuate from time to time from one person to another, as the problem requires. A tentative proposition to define in organisational terms the specifically scientific research organisation is therefore:

> ...a scientifically qualified work-group, oriented to the solution of a particular scientific problem, co-ordinated by the requirements of the technical and intellectual challenges, rather than by any hierarchy. Some division of labour takes place but may move from person to person as the problem suggests. Links with a corporate or university hierarchy are maintained through the director, but individual researchers are isolated from this hierarchy.

Such is the very great difference between models of organisation that exist in the literature and the model suggested here, which has been derived from the nature of scientific work, that one is drawn to conclude that the scientist has reason to fear the application of the existing model to science. It is feared, perhaps, because it is inappropriate. Attempts to apply it to science laboratories will only result in underachievement by science, and a decline in discovery and creativeness.

It would be naive to think that all laboratories are organised in ways that leave people equally free. New ideas can be seen in some organisations (research or otherwise) as dangerous; they threaten those whose careers and whose thinking are based on the old order of things. Machiavelli's (1513) comment on change may also apply to new ideas:

> ...there is nothing more difficult to execute, nor more dubious of success, nor more dangerous to administer than to introduce a new order of things; for he who introduces it has all those who profit from the old order as his enemies, and he has only lukewarm allies in all those who might profit from the new. This lukewarmness partly stems from fear of their adversaries, who have the law on their side, and partly from the scepticism of men, who do not truly believe in new things unless they have actually had experience of them. Therefore, it happens that whenever those who are enemies have the chance to attack, they do so enthusiastically, whereas those others defend hesitantly, so that they, together with the prince, are in danger.

Science is not devoid of critics of new ways of thinking. As long ago as the fifth century BC the Pythagoreans, incensed by the trouble that Hippasus' discovery of irrational numbers had caused them, are said to have taken him in a boat far out in the Mediterranean and thrown him overboard to die! There are many more modern examples of a reluctance to allow people to think freely and develop new ways of thinking.

Yet if a laboratory is to be effective, somehow ideas need to be encouraged without being seen as threats, but rather as contributions. Ideas that are emergent and tentative need to be carefully nourished, and ensured a warm climate in their infancy, as they can be very easily crushed in the budding. As the poet Yeats put it: 'Tread softly, for you tread on my dreams.'

Supervisors must be careful not to develop a climate of such critical appraisal that young researchers will only come out with ideas that are either basically conservative of the old schema of things, or none at all. Heinrich Rohrer is of the view:

> Certainly it turns out over the years that some people are more creative than others. But I think to a great extent creativity has been destroyed in most people, and not that it has been made in others.

All this presents a particular challenge to those supervising research, as they themselves may be under considerable pressure to produce results within a certain time-scale. Loehle (1990) points out that:

> The pressures on scientists today oppose truly creative thinking. Pressures to write grant proposals, teach, and publish, leave little time for undirected thinking. Industrial laboratories today are far more directed than in the past, particularly where costs per experiment are high.

Many studies have shown that freedom, for scientists, is a very important, perhaps essential, factor (Taylor and Sandler, 1973; Ekvall and Tangberg-Anderson, 1986; Amabile, 1988).

Can organisation be combined with freedom?

As we shall see, this freer form of research, outlined above in a commercial laboratory, but probably more usual in universities, does have a high degree of organisation, though this organisation is often invisible. Michael Polanyi, in a fascinating article called *The Republic of Science* (1962; excerpts reproduced by kind permission of Kluwer Academic Publishers), puts it as follows:

> ... scientists freely making their own choice of problems and pursuing them in the light of their own personal judgement are in fact co-operating as members of a closely knit organisation.

One might ask how it is possible for people 'freely making their own choice of problems in the light of their own personal judgement' to form a closely knit organisation. Polanyi explains this paradox:

> Imagine we are given the pieces of a very large jig-saw puzzle, and suppose for some reason, it is important that our giant puzzle be put together in the shortest possible time. We would naturally try to speed this up by engaging a number of helpers; the question is in what manner these could be best employed. Suppose we share out the pieces of the jig-saw puzzle equally among the helpers and let each of them work on his lot separately. It is easy to see that this method, which would be quite appropriate to a number of people shelling peas, would be totally ineffectual in this case, since few of the pieces allocated to one particular assistant would be found to fit together. We could do a little better by providing duplicates of all the pieces to each helper separately, and eventually somehow bring together their several results. But even by this method the team would not much surpass the performance of a single individual at his best. The only way the assistants can effectively co-operate and surpass by far what any single one of them could do, is to let them work on putting the puzzle together in sight of the others, so that every time a piece is fitted in by one helper, all the others will immediately watch out for the next step that becomes possible in consequence. Under this system, each helper will act on his own initiative, by responding to the latest achievements of the others, and the completion of their joint task will be greatly accelerated.
>
> We have here in a nutshell the way in which a series of independent initiatives are organised to a joint achievement by mutually adjusting themselves at every successive stage to the situation created by all the others who are acting likewise.

This appears to describe the approach taken by many Nobel laureates in their laboratories very well. They are not 'management by results' operations at all; rather, researchers used their own judgement, worked on what they thought best and shared it all in public view so that each colleague could learn from others. The invisible hand of co-ordination lay in the problem they all shared, rather than in tasks they had to perform.

Of course Polanyi's republic, like Plato's, works well only when given a number of assumptions. In order for this 'republic of science' to work, Polanyi admits one necessary assumption: that scientists keep making the best contribution of which they are capable, or, to put it in context, that scientists will make a better contribution under these circumstances than they would if they were managed and co-ordinated more closely. There are other assumptions it would be reasonable to make, including:

(a) that society at large encourages in its education programmes, and its shared values, freedom of thought in its members;
(b) that the best scientists of the available pool are selected;
(c) that scientists are well educated and trained;
(d) that all scientific knowledge is shared in the public domain;
(e) that projects are well thought out;
(f) that the research environment is conducive to this way of working;
(g) that adequate equipment and library support are available.

Some of these assumptions depend on society for their existence, others are within the control of the senior scientists in charge of each research project.

There are wider societal necessities which are not obvious, but which are clearly important. We have seen what must be the effect of these in Chapter 1, (Section 3) when the distribution of Nobel Prizes is outlined. Throughout the world, very few institutions in only a handful of countries attract these awards, and it would appear that most creative research emerges in these pockets.

The case against more closely controlled types of organisation is strongly made. These latter organisations often emphasise a focus on results, ironically at the expense of results. Polanyi (1962) states:

> Any attempt to organise the group of helpers under a single authority would eliminate their independent initiatives and thus reduce their joint effectiveness to that of the single person directing from the centre. It would, in effect, paralyse their co-operation.

Polanyi's idea is an attempt to provide a framework of freedom for the individual scientists, and yet retain co-ordination of the thrust and direction of the research at some macro level. His idea is perhaps somewhat idealistic, but is accurately descriptive as a model of international scientific research. Indeed, the advent of the information 'superhighway' has made his idea considerably more practical than at the time it was proposed.

The Human Genome Project provides an example of the balancing of directed research goals and experimental freedom. Among the immediate objectives of this project are complete genetic and physical mapping of the human genome, facilitating the localisation of disease genes. The approaches to these objectives have included various university-based groups working on different single chromosomes and a large French institute working intensively on genetically mapping the entire genome. While the specific goals of the project, such as the density and connectedness of the mapped genetic markers, were specified by the agencies funding the project, the experimental techniques to be employed for this mapping were not. In fact, one rationale for conducting the mapping of single chromosomes at different universities:

> ...was that a multifaceted, multi-university approach would identify the optimal experimental strategies, rather than placing all eggs in one basket. Furthermore, the funding of several groups would spread the money and technology around, preventing the creation of a single specialised centre (Hoffman, 1994).

In other words, by allowing scientists the freedom to develop their own approaches to a well-defined problem, it is hoped that they will do more than apply existing techniques to fill in experimental details (which would fall into the realm of 'normal science'). Much of the Genome Project could well be described as 'normal science', though discovery may emerge in a variety of aspects of it, including in the development of innovative experimental approaches and techniques. The Genome Project has specific goals set at a wide international level, but allows individual scientists total freedom in their approaches to the solution of each aspect.

Normally regarded as less organised, university laboratories appear to be more creative (although they considerably outnumber industry-based laboratories). Without carefully planned research, we do not know which of these two systems (the free or the managed) actually works better, or how much possible creative discovery actually never takes place, for reasons related to control and freedom. Heinrich Rohrer, a participant in this study, cautions us:

> It is simply an assumption that project supervisors and doctoral thesis supervisors try to do their best to create the right spirit for creative science, but I simply would not take it for granted. The existence of real dedication to scientific endeavour is a very rare thing. Where it does occur, and where the supervisor is dedicated, and happens to select good, intelligent students, that is all that is necessary for good research to be done. We probably more readily destroy creativity, more than we foster it. I believe we should watch more what we are doing in destroying creativity, than we need to consider ways of promoting it.

Even outside the area of scientific research, organisations realise this weakness, and have attempted to alter organisational systems and structures, in order to allow bounded freedom to creative people. The term 'bounded freedom' is used here to indicate that unlimited freedom is not a reality. Conceptual frameworks such as the 'facilitating organisation' described by Hurley (1982) can be useful in considering the way in which organisation must accommodate and change in order to retain control and direction, on the one hand, and, on the other, to encourage the creative abilities of organisational members in their work. Other concepts such as those of 'empowerment' and 'learning organisations' suggest the development of organisations that become adaptive to changing work requirements. In other words, it is possible for the organisational environment of the research laboratory to act in such a way that creativity will either flourish or be discouraged.

Non-organisational limitations

It is not only the organisation that may restrict scientists' freedom of thought. Sometimes, the very extent and depth of existing scientific knowledge can act as a brake on new forms of thinking about and reframing problems. Rohrer is of the opinion that there are essential tensions (which can constrain freedom of thought) between the forces of the body of knowledge, on the one hand, and the desire to approach something new, on the other:

> Perhaps the scientific method constrains us and we should be freer to think in a freer framework. But I think that's unavoidable because you have to learn first what actually exists. Of course if you take that which exists as the full truth, then when the crucial moment comes, what you have learned, though you have to take it as the truth, yet not everything of it is the full truth. Maybe we should learn more and more under what circumstances this is the case, and how it should be. That is why we use experiments and also use a theoretical framework. An experiment only makes sense when you also give the circumstances under which you have done the experiment. Under these conditions very often something is established. Newtonian mechanics explained much of the world we knew, but the known world is now larger, so classical mechanics, though inadequate, is not in principle wrong. If you think classical mechanics is wrong because quantum mechanics is different, then I think one makes a mistake; one should look at classical mechanics as a special case of quantum mechanics. In fact, if you think about it, maybe quantum mechanics might be a special case of something which would allow us to approach complexity, and all complex systems such as the biological system in a more natural way, in a more effective way. But we simply have to be aware that quantum mechanics is not the end of wisdom, lets put it that way.

This extract shows very clearly how a successful scientist is not constrained by the existing framework of thought. He looks at science as a continuous, unfolding process of discovery, and sees himself as an explorer open to surprises and welcoming of new landfalls. However, there is a conservative tendency in the way people think, which tends to regard the existing structures of what is known in science as the complete and final story. Logically, of course, we know that this is not so, but much of what is constructed in theory and tested in experimentation and application has such a 'right' look about it that we can easily fall into the trap of thinking within that framework and forgetting that it is only a step along the way, our present best guess. The ability to know the whole structure of our field, and yet have the freedom to find defects and anomalies within it, is at the very core of scientific creativity. This dichotomy was referred to as 'creative tension' by Kuhn (1962). Later Pelz and Andrews' (1966) studies of scientists in organisations brought him a similar conclusion:

... technical men were effective when faced with some general demand from the environment, when their associates held divergent viewpoints, or the laboratory climate required some disruption of established patterns.

Intellectual freedom is often thought of negatively by those responsible for research, who may think of 'divergent viewpoints' as steps towards chaos. They sometimes view freedom as meaning a licence to go down unproductive routes or to waste valuable project time by ill-considered explorations of unlikely areas, of little relation to the topic being studied. Of course this may be the case, but freedom of thought is so important to the dedicated scientist that attempts to 'co-ordinate' the research closely can easily result in the researcher of excellence leaving the project and the more organisationally malleable people (who may not require such independence and freedom) remaining.

The possible role of organisation in relation to the provision of freedom and the maximisation of the possibilities provided by chance is explored in Chapter 6 in the sections on 'capitalising on chance' and cultivating serendipity'.

Chapter 6

Some Considerations on the Organisation of Discovery-Related Science

1 INTRODUCTION

In the foregoing chapters, an attempt has been made to show that organisation may be an important and neglected dimension in scientific discovery. In Chapter 7, suggestions are made as to how this hypothesis might be tested empirically. By way of illustrating the possible role of various aspects of organisation in scientific excellence, three key aspects of organisation in relation to science are explored.

This chapter is an attempt to show the nature of organisational factors in relation to discovery. The argument that has been built up in previous chapters shows that most science is a group activity, taking place within an organisational context. The solving, even the finding and framing, of scientific problems depends on the collaboration of scientists in a particular field of study.

This is not to diminish the central role of the individual in arriving at insights, but rather to point to the fact that most individual scientists work not alone but as active members of a research group, which itself exists in an organisational setting. They are each autonomous groups, and most experiments are carried out in such groups. The development and honing of scientific understanding is carried out with one's colleagues. Only in certain forms of science — mathematics and theoretical physics for example — does the role of the scientific group seem less important.

Scientists are often not particularly aware of the contribution of the organisation (be it the society in which they are born, state support for science or university support for their projects) because most frequently the organisation is actually *invisible* to the scientists. From the individual scientist's point of view this invisibility of the organisation is probably necessary to protect him or her from becoming excessively involved in administration, which is not their career. The invisible nature of that which has supported them frees them to be creative, when, if it was otherwise, it could sidetrack them and be harmful to their creative energy. However, from the viewpoint of those concerned with the organisation of science, in particular the facilitation of creative science, this organisation cannot be invisible. It must be studied, examined and experimented with, for otherwise the organisational determinants of creative science cannot be established, and the possibility would not exist to replicate those conditions where they do not at present exist.

How exactly might the group or the organisation affect the world of the scientist? Most fundamentally, it is the organisation that attracts, selects and employs the young scientist. After selection, once the scientist has joined the laboratory, he or she becomes affected by the organisational climate. This climate affects morale, not just of the scientist but of everyone else in the laboratory. Technicians and research assistants are affected by morale and, depending on the situation, can be more or less enthusiastic about the research. Unwittingly, perhaps, the young scientist joining a research group can be strongly affected by these matters.

Then of course the leadership, enthusiasm and sheer organisational ability of the principal investigator can also affect the young scientist. All of this depends very importantly on the organisational resources available to the research project and can be a key factor in making good research possible. In this chapter, an overview is given of those organisational aspects that may play a significant part in affecting the process of scientific discovery. They are: the selection of discoverer-scientists, the dynamics of research groups and the organisational role in capitalising on chance in research.

2 THE SELECTION OF DISCOVERER-SCIENTISTS

Characteristics of discoverer-scientists

As we have already seen in Chapter 1, discovery appears to be dependent on a variety of factors, both personal (such as education) and institutional (such as the organisation and dynamics of the research group). In considering how scientists might be selected, one of the main aims of the procedures used should be to provide a pool of scientists with a high probability of contributing to discovery. If selection methods could achieve this objective, they would be of considerable importance to the principle investigator.

Self-selection by reward preference

It is possible that the pool of potential scientists is to some extent self-selected on the basis of reward preference. Those science graduates with a preference for immediate monetary reward will enter banking or marketing, or some organisation exploiting scientific results for the market. On the other hand, it is likely that those who opt for a career in science will be interested in a different set of rewards. They will know that the rewards are rather different in science to those available in industry. Financial rewards for on-going research are usually modest, but the thrill of the chase and the fascination of a certain area in science, and of course the possibility that an important contribution will be made, are powerful stimulants to the dedicated researcher.

According to Root-Bernstein (1994):

> Another practical implication of recognizing that each stage of research requires different personality types is that you need to reward each type of individual appropriately. It is a common mistake to take exploratory scientists and reward their insights by promoting them to head of a group devoted to developing their discovery. Explorer's don't want to do the tedious developmental work. They hate it. Reward them instead by either giving them more freedom or putting them in charge of their own exploratory group (or 'skunk works') where their scientific and personality skills will be most appropriate. Conversely, you can't expect developmental or applications experts to have the risk-taking, qualitative, incomplete approach to research that characterizes the pioneer. They won't make good members of exploratory teams, nor will they do well as their managers.

The rewards available to laboratories for excellence in research are most usually not financial. They take the form of promotion, acclaim or honours, and the estimation of colleagues. In some cases, the knowledge that one has contributed to curing some disease can also be a powerful reward. According to Blumberg:

> The students chosen for doctoral and post-doctoral work should have a kind of passion for their work and know that their work is their life.

In other words, it is not money or fame which excites excellent scientists, but the intriguing character of the work that is research. The identification of this passion at the selection stage is difficult, though perhaps not impossible.

How the Nobel laureates were selected

To get to know more about their views on selection, two questionnaires were completed by the Nobel laureates, and this subject formed part of the interview. The first questionnaire asked for their views on how they themselves were selected and what aspects of the procedure used were considered most important. The second questionnaire asked them to indicate the importance of several factors used by them for current selection. Their responses on selection questionnaire A gave the results shown in Table 9.

All the other areas listed in the questionnaire were either never used, as in the following examples:

Table 9 The Nobel laureates' view of the importance of certain factors in their own selection

	Mean	Standard error of mean
The view of the search committee	4.00	—
Evidence of a very high ability	4.00	0.00
The interview	3.83	0.17
References	3.83	0.17
A current supervisor's assessment	3.67	0.33
Their judgement of your previous work	3.50	0.34
The quality of your publications	3.60	0.40
Your colleague's assessment	3.57	0.30
Biographical data	3.17	0.31
Your own future autobiography	3.00	0.00
Your performance during a trial period in your laboratory	3.00	—
The grade of your primary degree in science	3.00	0.55
The quantity of your publications	2.67	0.33
The results of specific tests of scientific ability	2.00	—
The results of specific tests of scientific creativity	2.00	—
Your self-assessment	2.20	0.58

(a) evidence of very high ability (e.g. GMAT or SAT scores),
(b) results of specific tests of scientific ability,
(c) results of specific tests of scientific creativity,

or they were given scores that indicated the respondent's view that these areas lacked importance. These were:

(a) their self-assessment,
(b) view of search committee,
(c) their own future autobiography.

Given these results from the questionnaire, the Nobel laureates made useful comments in their discussions on both how they themselves were selected and the role of various components of the selection process in selecting scientists of talent. It is noteworthy that the interview is placed first in importance in this rank-ordering. Analysis of the discussions which took place with the Nobel laureates suggests that this is because most of the individuals in this study actually approached the laboratory they first worked in, and after a brief discussion (interview) started work there. The process by which these very talented scientists joined their laboratories is probably 'a road less travelled by' than the route most usually used by scientists. Most are selected using the methods described below, and of course most scientists work in 'normal' science and do not themselves make significant discoveries (even though they may be an essential contributor). However, the scientists in this study, who have been acknowledged by their peers as contributing to science in a highly significant way, seem to have approached their laboratories in rather unique ways. There may be many reasons for this, but the one for which we have the most evidence is the great clarity these people have about their work. They seem to possess more knowledge, and at an earlier age, of the nature of the problems which face science, and also have a very clear idea of their role in it. With this as part of their personality, it seems that those in this study often knew exactly whom they would like to work with and approached that person. That scientist also formed the impression quickly that the young scientist who had approached him was a person of high scientific motivation, and employed him or her immediately. It is likely that this process of accurate selection by the young scientist also took account of the nature of the laboratory, its resources, its place in a prestigious university or commercial organisation and the presence of colleagues of considerable ability and renown.

It would seem from these views that most Nobel laureates were attracted to their laboratories, as distinct from selected. Indeed, Porter, Lawler and Hackman (1975) describe a heuristic which allows for the organisation to attract the individual or the individual to attract the organisation. All the Nobel laureates in this study had joined prestigious and well-endowed laboratories at an early stage in their career. They were attracted primarily by the nature and quality of the research being carried out in those laboratories. This attraction can be illustrated by looking at that early stage when they were seeking their first paid employment. Most had become very interested in a certain scientific field, indeed a rather precise part of a field. Having developed this interest, and being well informed, they had by then identified a key figure in that field and made themselves known to that person. This person found these scientists attractive, too, because they had a clearly expressed interest in their own field and had a good university record. The first job that Richard Ernst took is a case in point. He had seen the instruments produced by Varian in California and thought that if they could make such fine instruments, they must really be exceptional. So when it came to getting his first job:

> ... after my studies, I wanted to leave the university for ever; I did not intend ever to come back. I found the academic atmosphere sterile and it was difficult for me to find a sufficiently strong motivation to do research for its own sake. This was the reason why I wanted to go to industry. For my postdoctoral years in the United States, I selected ten possible companies and visited them on a trip through the USA. None of them truly pleased me, many performed rather low level science. All of them were too much oriented towards solving minor daily problems, so to say the other extreme in comparison to the work at the university. So I decided on an eleventh company which I did not visit: Varian Associates, where I knew that they combine science and engineering in a very creative way. And I was not disappointed. I met in Dr Weston Anderson a truly ideal boss with almost unlimited creativity and an extraordinarily nice person. I found an extremely

creative atmosphere which I found very stimulating. I still do not know how I had deserved the luck to work under such ideal circumstances.

Ernst was attracted to a smaller but high calibre company in preference to larger, more established ones. Herbert Brown, too, had proved attractive to those running an important scientific project:

The National Defence Research Committee was farming out various projects to various professors and schools to do, and one of them came to Professor Slezenger. He asked me to drop my normal academic work and work on this project.

Hewish had a similar experience as he was graduating:

I had not planned to do research at all. I had got a job all lined up with what was then called the College of Aeronautics in Cranfield. It is now a university. When the people in my department at Cambridge heard about it, they said why don't you stay in Cambridge to do research. That seemed a nice idea. So I just talked around and radio astronomy was about the one field that had any vacancies at that stage. I'm not sure it was even called radio astronomy then. The fact that you could pick up radio waves from outer space was known, and research was being carried out in the Cavendish. I did not know that, even as a student, but I knew the person doing it, Martin Ryall, with whom I worked during the war on electronic devices, so it seemed a good idea to stay on. I got in as a real clean hand into this, and spent my first year getting experiments and designing antennas.

Geoffrey Wilkinson had a similar experience:

In December 1942 I was recruited for the Atomic Energy Commission in Canada and sent out there. I have no idea why I was selected except that I was top of my year in 1942.

Baruch Blumberg was also approached:

In 1957 I was completing my graduate studies at Oxford University Department of Biochemistry when I received several letters from medical research establishments in the United States. One of these was from the Division of Clinical Research of the National Institutes of Health, Bethesda, Maryland, offering me a position as a Senior Investigator. I accepted this and started my employment in 1957 after the award of my DPhil degree (I had received my MD degree in 1951).

It is clear that, for many scientists, a selection process in the usual sense was not used. Rather, a process of mutual discovery of talented and enthusiastic young graduates, by key scientists, took place. In most cases this was the result of an earlier decision to become involved in a particular area of study for their doctoral work. Having researched deeply in this area, they had of course identified the key laboratories and key researchers in this field. They then made their approach, mutual recognition took place and they started work in that laboratory. It is clear that this approach strategy which they used is quite

Table 10   The Nobel laureates' view of the importance of certain factors in current selection practices

	Mean	Standard error of mean
A current supervisor's assessment	3.82	0.12
Their colleagues' assessment	3.80	0.20
Your judgement of their previous work	3.73	0.14
The interview	3.70	0.15
The view of the search committee	3.67	0.33
References	3.64	0.20
Their colleagues' assessment	3.60	0.22
The quality of their publications	3.55	0.21
Their performance during a trial period in your laboratory	3.25	0.25
The grade of their primary degree	3.11	0.20
Evidence of their ability	3.00	0.00
Their own future autobiography	3.00	0.00
Their self-assessment	2.63	0.38
The quantity of their publications	2.33	0.37
The results of specific tests of scientific ability	2.00	—
The results of specific tests of scientific creativity	2.00	—

different from the selection process used in most other work situations. It seems likely that this will continue to be the preferred mode of entry of very talented scientists into their long term employment. The implications for those laboratories that wish to have such people working with them are clear.

Current selection practice puts quite a different emphasis on aspects of the selection procedure. There is less reliance on the interview (though it is still considered very important) but biographical data, the panel's judgement of their previous work and colleagues' assessment have become more important. The Nobel laureates seem to prefer to select on the basis of more measurable aspects of a scientist's work (see Table 10) than those which formed the basis of their own subjectivity. Yet there is considerable agreement among the laureates, that the interview is an important method of assessing the creative aspect of a scientist's personality, and cannot be omitted.

Hewish described the Cavendish Laboratory approach as follows:

> We select our research students by examination and interview. There is a top ten per cent selection immediately by examination, but whether we accept them or not is down to interview. And we either like them or we don't like them. You try to assess brightness, knowledge — not too much knowledge — because to get to that level they know some stuff. That does not mean to say they are going to be very creative. You can ask them questions as to whether they understand what they are doing rather than just being bookworms; and whether they are enthusiastic, what they have done in the past and get to know them as people.... We are looking for this creative thing; being bright does not necessarily mean they have got the

research outlook. You can find potential creativity by the enthusiasm shown by the students, by the sort of thing they do and say about those aspects of physics they don't understand. By giving them a problem to think about which they won't have found in the textbooks. That's what research is—you can't look it up in a book.... The interview is a blunt instrument but it does show something. They have got to show some liveliness and sparkle. (I would, however, have probably rejected myself on those grounds!)

Benacerraf's view is:

Scientists are selected on the basis of their past record, recommendations and especially a lengthy interview. I try to ascertain the motivation of the applicant and their commitment to a lifetime career in science. This plus high intelligence and the capacity for hard work are the necessary requirements.

Gertrude Elion also attaches great importance to the interview:

I put great weight on the interview to judge enthusiasm, understanding, interest in the work and the ability to ask the appropriate questions. The 'gleam in the eye' was always a major factor for me. I was also very interested in knowing what people really wanted to do, since I am a firm believer in being happy in your work. It would be foolish to give a person a job in which they would be unhappy or uncomfortable.

Frederick Sanger:

If possible, (candidates) usually came for an interview. Most were post docs from abroad, so I usually had to rely on references. I considered their personality was important. Would they fit in well with me and other members of the staff?

Though they seem to have moved to requiring greater behavioural evidence of scientific research ability, yet there is no desire to downgrade the interview. Rather, it is seen as the only way to get some (however subjective) idea as to the future discovery potential of each candidate. It is important to bear in mind that the interview as carried out by a person of known exceptional contribution may well be qualitatively different from one carried out by other scientists. Those scientists involved in research that has led to discovery are perhaps more likely to recognise the creative spark in other scientists. This is an area where very fruitful research could be conducted.

Degree levels

The Nobel laureates were by no means certain that degree level was an important factor in selecting scientists with an orientation towards discovery. Though all of those interviewed had themselves achieved distinction in their undergraduate degrees, they had experienced working with scientists with a wide level of qualification, and were not convinced of a relationship between degree level and creativity or discovery in research. Geoffrey Wilkinson was blunt:

First class honours have got absolutely nothing to do with capabilities of doing good research. You have either got the ability or you do not.

Frederick Sanger stressed devotion to a lifetime of dedicated research:

Regarding selection for doctoral work, it is not ideal to select people on the basis of a first class degree or a strong second. The thing you really need is someone who is going to be devoted to the subject and is interested in it. I do not think that you can measure that. You can, however, get an idea from their personality, whether they will become better or not.

This entry process is truly definitive in deciding which individual will work in the field of science research, and at what level. It is also the decisive step for science itself in determining the proportion of especially talented minds that is drawn into the field, at any given time. It is particularly important that this process be carried out effectively, since there are always dangers which would reduce the numbers of people entering a field who are likely to make discoveries, including the danger of selecting scientists simply because they are similar to the selectors. This 'comfortable' option could be very disruptive to the future of scientific development. Most applicants may well be competent, but competence alone does not mean that those selected will also be really creative.

From Herbert Brown comes a suggestion that certain tests could predict discovery in science:

I have observed that the best chemists are those who speak and write very clearly. When I get their graduate records in, the most important thing there is the language score. The chemistry or the quantitative score is of secondary importance to me. ... I have found apparently, that the same qualities of the mind that allow people to formulate the language to express things clearly are those that enable them to formulate research and do it in a systematic excellent manner. We have found through the analysis of past records at Purdue University, that the best chemists are those who did very well in the verbal component of the GRE exam. We have found a marked correlation.

The effective selection of scientists

The effectiveness (or otherwise) of a process of selection lies in its predictive power. A process of selection will be judged to be effective to the extent to which it selects candidates who perform significantly better than others (selected by some other process), when performing the jobs for which they have been selected. Smith and Robertson (1989) have shown that the closer the assessment procedure gets to sampling a person's actual performance on related work, (the work sample) the better the validity. By contrast, those very methods used almost exclusively in science, the references and the interview, have been shown to have disturbingly low levels of validity. It would seem that a clear preliminary case exists for selection into scientific research positions to be carried out using methods that have been shown (admittedly in other areas of work) to be more effective. Instead of using methods whose validity is low, such as the interview or the references, there could be a case made for a move to those methods where the validity has been shown to be high (e.g. the work sample, composite ability measures). When research scientists are selected, the validated processes outlined tend not to be adopted, and very little research has been published on the selection criteria that are employed. Thus, information on the predictive ability of the criteria which are in use is largely unknown. Some studies have been carried out to explore this possible predictive power. Jones, cited in Guilford (1967a), in a study based on 100 engineers and scientists, found correlations of 0.54 between rated creativity and Guilford's consequences and 0.34 for ideational fluency. One study was carried out in the Netherlands to validate a test battery for the selection of research scientists (Elshout *et al.*, 1973). This study took place among 184 scientific researchers under 40 years old, who had worked for more than two years in their laboratory. As a criterion, five raters were asked to rate each researcher; they were: the direct boss (S1), the department head (S2), a colleague involved in the same research (C1), another colleague (C2) and the researcher himself or herself (Z). The raters were asked to rate each researcher on 17 scales, each relating to important aspects of their behaviour. A battery of tests of creativity based on Guilford's (1967a) model were administered to each researcher. This study indicates the kind of research that is needed which would, however, (use discovery rather than creativity as a criterion). A useful study along these lines would include a variety of scientists, including those who are agreed to be significant discoverers. This study is important in that it showed, firstly, that creativity has a number of components and, secondly, that certain tests can predict creativity with a reasonable degree of reliability. Combinations of the tests were found to predict each of the four factors with multiple correlations as high as 0.8 (Elshout *et al.*, 1973). There are very few studies such as this, and there is a need for more on these lines. If we cannot accurately predict discovery in science we might just as well continue to select scientists in the same way as we do currently. After all, current practice is speedy and inexpensive. Its disadvantage is that it may not select those people science has most need of—scientists with truly original minds. Hence, if we are to use some other method of selection, that method must be shown to have some probable advantage over the existing method. In fact, the effectiveness of this decisive process in science is largely unknown. When industry selects a manager or a computer programmer, for example, it is quite usual for an elaborate process of recruitment to be undertaken. This process usually begins with an advertising campaign to make sure that the largest number of qualified candidates is aware of the position being advertised. This proceeds to a short-listing on the basis of carefully evaluated criteria or using standardised testing procedures. The procedure then continues through to the interview process, which is itself so organised as to maximise objective evaluation (i.e. by structured interviews and panel interviews). In addition, potential candidates occasionally go to assessment centres where they may spend some days being evaluated over a wide range of social, psychological and behavioural indicators. Selected candidates are then appointed (usually on a probationary basis, in order to facilitate their further evaluation) and go through an induction session in order to ensure a smooth assimilation into the organisation.

This process is subsequently evaluated in the light of the selected employee's contribution to the organisation's objectives. The usual process in relation to most research positions in universities or institutes is that notices are simply placed on university notice boards or circulated to forthcoming graduates through careers and appointments offices in the same university. These often originate as temporary contract positions and later become permanent jobs. In some cases, the positions are advertised in local scientific publications or newsletters, or in national newspapers.

The impression one gets is that for every one position that is advertised, perhaps ten have been filled in this rather informal way. Relatively few positions are advertised in other countries, except where they are adjacent and speak the same language. It is also most usually stated or at least widely known that candidates will not be selected unless they have a first class honours degree or its equivalent. This equivalent might include, for example, a second class honours degree plus a strong recommendation from the Head of Department or some evidence of publication or unusually developed experimental skills. It is most unusual for any attempt to be made to evaluate these selection decisions. Indeed, a proper evaluation of these decisions would require a scientifically designed longitudinal study, comparing experimental with control groups. It would involve the experimental selection of candidates across the full range from first class honours to pass degrees, and a subsequent evaluation against objective criteria of performance in the research projects for which they were selected. Indeed, the development of adequate criteria for success in scientific work might prove to be the most difficult aspect of this research. It is a strange irony that in a discipline as exact as science research, probably the most important single step that a department or a research project ever takes (that of selecting its members) is carried out so casually, and without adequate review. Of course, scientists given charge of considerable research funds will in some cases take expert advice or read textbooks on selection before making any decisions, but the impression from science research departments across a number of universities and countries is that this is unusual.

Texts on selection can be very useful guides indeed and the following can be recommended highly: Herriot (1989), Smith and Robertson (1989) and Armstrong (1991). However, no specific text exists at present which covers the rather specialised needs of the scientific community. This would appear to present most interesting selection and test research possibilities for work and organisational psychologists in collaboration with research laboratories, the aim of which would be to improve the success rate in selecting creative scientists. Current thinking in the area of selection sees the selection process as a starting point, a 'point of entry' (Herriot, 1989), in a much longer process of organisational assimilation. It is clear that all the Nobel laureates in this study, and probably most others, joined organisations and, in general, had good experiences. They were permitted that freedom so necessary to the scientist, provided with those resources (both human and technical) that they needed, and they were encouraged to grow and develop within their organisation. According to Drenth (1989):

> It would be extremely unwise to treat selection as an isolated phenomenon and to dissociate it from the general organisational personnel system. Selection should be conceived as a first and integral phase in the total career guidance system of personnel in the organisation.

Clearly this has not been the case for all scientists. It is even possible that many universities and commercial laboratories got their selection right, and then proceeded to treat a potentially highly creative scientist so badly that his or her potential was never realised. Effective selection depends on the existence of effective predictors. A number of selection techniques are available, the use of which allows us to select from a pool of applicants those most likely to be successful in science, however we decide to measure such success.

The use of psychological tests in the selection of discoverer-scientists

In a fascinating chapter, Hocevar and Bachelor (1989) classify more than 100 examples of creativity measurement. They subdivide these tests into eight categories as follows:

   (i) Tests of divergent thinking
  (ii) Attitude and interest inventories
 (iii) Personality inventories
 (iv) Biographical inventories
  (v) Ratings by teachers, peers and supervisors
 (vi) Judgements of products
(vii) Eminence
(viii) Self-reported creative activities and achievements

In their evaluation of these various approaches, Hocevar and Bachelor (1989) conclude that:

Research that has the most bearing on what society recognizes as actual creativity can best be accomplished studying eminent women and men, analysing creative products and administering inventories of creative activities and accomplishments.

They find that most of the other measures listed above are too easily confused with other related abilities such as intelligence and verbal fluency, but may not in fact be related to creativity in science.

Guilford *et al.* (1951–1956) review numerous tests for high level ability and conclude that most of them are related to convergent thinking; for each item there is one correct answer. True tests of creative ability should surely look for the exact opposite: divergent, novel solutions to problems. Hudson (1966), whose sample was based on highly intelligent boys in senior college and freshmen at college found that existing intelligence tests failed to distinguish between the ordinary capable student and the outstandingly creative one. Even tests which are divergent such as those developed by McKinnon *et al.* (1960) do not seem to distinguish between the truly creative person and the average. To validly predict creative scientific ability, we need to know what are the characteristics displayed by people with such ability. We know that creative scientists need to have high ability in the following areas:

● General intelligence
● Specific scientific ability
● High levels of persistence
● High ability to develop hypotheses

The first two of these abilities are probably tested adequately during undergraduate courses, and perseverance as we have seen may be inferred from a variety of life activities which are continued and developed over long periods of time. Frederiksen and Ward (1973) have developed a test for measuring a scientist's ability to generate hypotheses by presenting a set of data, having the scientist applicant develop a set of hypotheses for the data and having these rated by a scientific team. The evaluations are carried out for:

● The number of hypotheses
● The number of acceptable hypotheses
● The quality of the hypotheses
● Their scaled value
● The number of words in each hypothesis

Though this test appears to have promise, work on them appears to have been discontinued, and no separate versions for the various physical sciences have been developed.

Following on from the Wallas (1926) heuristic, preparation, incubation, illumination, verification, which describes the processes of science research,

they propose a series of work samples to be taken from one field of science —
psychology — as follows:

- Measuring psychological constructs
- Formulating research ideas
- Analysing psychological constructs
- Evaluating hypotheses
- Evaluating proposals
- Ideational fluency in psychology
- Scanning speed (of scientific articles)

This appears to present a useful framework for the development of predictive
tests in any scientific field.

The interview

Since it is likely that the interview will continue to be used in selecting
scientists, its effectiveness should be properly evaluated. The nature of the
interview should also be more defined than it often is. An interview is often
simply a 'cosy chat', the objective of which is unclear. Current thinking in
selection research suggests that the closer the interview replicates the work
situation, the more useful will it be in predicting subsequent performance. The
interview, could therefore be highly structured and use evaluation forms to
check the candidate's interest or enthusiasm for science. According to Elion:

> I paid quite a bit of attention to selection. I think this a critical thing in choosing
> people: I told (candidates) about the work I was doing, and I watched their
> reactions. I wanted to see if they lit up, and that is the only way I can describe it. If
> they understand what I am telling them, they ask a question or two, they show
> enthusiasm, they don't just sit there like a bump on a log. If you tell them
> something that you think is exciting, and they don't react, I don't want them. They
> have to get some inkling as to what kind of work we are doing and they have to
> think it is a good idea, and be excited about it.

Elion was not keen on having a 'bump on a log' working with her, but rather
someone with that spark of enthusiasm which is so valuable in science. The
interview could also explore the candidate's ability to suggest hypotheses, their
awareness of current scientific problems and their ability to design and organise
experiments. An emphasis on these abilities rather than personality variables
could give a more constructive focus to the interview, and would also improve
its reliability as a predictor of later work.

It would indeed be desirable if we could predict discovery in science by way
of a test, perhaps a test of creativity, coupled with evidence of persistence. The
availability of such a selection tool would increase the probability of effective
and creative research within each project. However, many of the tests
developed so far have relied on criteria that are less than appropriate in the

serious matter of selecting a research scientist. They have been based on criteria such as remote associations, associations far from the obvious (Mednick, 1962, 1963), ideational fluency, which may not relate to the precise field of science, or Guilford's unusual uses for familiar objects. These tests have often been validated on children, on student populations or on scientists whose creativity is unknown. To date, the main problem in validating tests of creativity in science has been the absence of agreement on suitable criteria. For any test, four types of validity exist. These are: face validity, content validity or the extent to which a test includes a sample of the domain being tested, construct validity where the test is shown to measure a theoretical construct related to the field and criterion validity where performance on the test can be related to performance in real life. The type of validity which may well show the most promise is the last. Two kinds of criteria can be used to validate tests in this criterion-based way: the first is objective measures of productivity, some of which may be creative; the second is ratings by scientific colleagues in the same field. Both have to be validated on well-established creative scientists, and if tests are developed in this way, they could be effectively used in the selection of younger scientists. In most cases, the same measures could not be applied to young applicants, as their record of achievement thus far is likely to be in relation to their academic development. Distinctions and publications are likely to have been few. Objective measures of the productivity of scientists include the number of citations in related refereed journals. This listing is given in the Science Citation Index and reports the importance of the works cited in the view of colleagues and may or may not be related to the number of publications by the author. In any case, usually a small number of articles by a given author are cited widely. The number of citations is in fact the best predictor of scientific honours, including the Nobel prizes (Ashton and Oppenheim, 1978), and there is a strong correlation between number of publications and number of citations (see, for example, Cole and Cole, 1967). The publications of many well-known scientists support this finding. According to Simonton (1988b), Darwin had 119 publications by the end of his career, Einstein 248, Galton 227 and Freud 330. Clearly, the notion that famous scientists were those who had one great insight is incorrect. In fact, as the above list of citations indicates, quality is also accompanied by quantity. Cole and Cole (1967) found that the average number of publications by Nobel laureates was 58, when the average for all scientists was 5.5!

Best selection practice

As we have seen in Chapter 1, most institutions have not received Nobel prizes, nor have they enjoyed the reputations for excellence that those institutions which have Nobel laureates do. Hence it is possible that the selection characteristics in these institutions is different from those practised in most others. The present study is confined to that subset of the institutions which do attract Nobel prizes, though fortunately it is a fairly large subset. Discussions on the topic of selection of scientists with each of those interviewed revealed what appears to be a series of common practices, some but not all of which may be replicable elsewhere. It is very likely, for example, that the very fact of their high world reputation for excellence will ensure a large applicant pool. A high proportion of these applicants are likely also to be of high intelligence, have high motivation levels and have adequate ego-strength. The central nature of the selection process in science research and the often haphazard way by which it is carried out has been outlined in this chapter. The multi-faceted nature of science research, with its unpredictable outcomes and its objectives (which are difficult to define), has been delineated. The diverse nature of scientists themselves has been explored. In particular, their personality types and their considerable need for passion and perseverance have been dealt with. The many differing approaches to selection which take place in university and other laboratories have been summarised. If an approach to research into the selection of scientists were based on what has been learned in the studies referred to here, it would be a start in the process of understanding the nature of the requirements we have for scientists of differing kinds to work in different research projects.

3 THE DYNAMICS OF RESEARCH GROUPS

Morale

Many scientists enter laboratories with more or less equally high levels of creativity, persistence and intelligence, but meet with very different organisational learning experiences in those laboratories. These experiences are very much the responsibility of the principal investigator, and indirectly of the organisation.

One chemistry PhD described two very different experiences. The first was in a physiology lab at an East Coast medical school:

The principal investigator maintained a small but dedicated staff of about half a dozen technicians and students ... (and) ... 'kept in touch' with her colleagues. The principal investigator participated in every phase. Students in the research group were personally instructed by the principal investigator, who not only made it clear that she was always available to answer questions big and small, but also emphasized the skills, areas of expertise, and availability of the technicians as sources of advice or information. A set of coherent research goals and a plan for achieving them had been communicated to each member of the lab. Everyone understood the hypotheses which were being tested. Everyone had a rich enough background, thanks to lunch time chats and constant communication with the principal investigator, to be able to identify unexpected results which might prove important. No one felt that his or her task was isolated from possible discovery. Moreover, everyone took a turn participating in each aspect of the studies, so the interconnection between tasks was well understood. Unusual results were discussed immediately, and innovative experimental techniques were suggested and tried frequently. The group's attention to detail and grasp of the big picture resulted in much solid data, numerous publications and invited talks at conferences, and plentiful grant funding. There was a general feeling in this laboratory that good and exciting science was being done (Stemwedel, 1994).

Later in her undergraduate career, she had quite a different experience in a pharmacology lab, which serves to illustrate the effect differing methods of organisation can have on the individual researcher:

This research group was a crowded one, with more than two dozen students and technicians working in two small laboratories. During my nine months in this research lab, I spoke to the principal investigator perhaps half a dozen times, and never about the rationale for my experiments or for the projects of the research group as a whole. The principal investigator ... never set foot in the laboratories. My training was left to two of the technicians, ... (who) were unable to answer questions about difficulties of particular cell lines or advantages or disadvantages of different types of growing media, and they were unaware of sources of information which might answer such questions. Safety precautions were either presented as an afterthought, or were ignored altogether. No one had even a hunch why the compounds he or she was testing were good candidates for anti-cancer treatments. More than one technician commented about feeling like a machine which generated data for the principal investigator to digest. Since no attempt was made by the principal investigator to communicate the grand scheme into which each experiment fits, lab members understood neither the importance of each other's experiments, nor the possible interconnections between different experiments.... technicians and students evaluated their progress on the basis of the sheer volume of data produced. Possible errors, if recognized at all, were not reported, since these would represent a set-back in time and in the amount of data one had been able to present. Since the principal investigator was entirely absent from the lab, she had no way to identify from the data which ended up on her desk which experiments were performed competently and which were not (Stemwedel, 1994).

It would seem clear that the scientists' experiences can be quite different, and in some cases quite harmful, to the development of experimental skills and theoretical thinking. At least this science student's first experience was a good one. What might have happened had the bad experience been her first one?

Whereas no study for scientists exists on these lines, an interesting longitudinal study of managerial careers was carried out by Howard and Bray (1988) in AT&T. This study followed up on managers for up to 20 years after they joined the company and linked their promotion (or lack of it) with various measures and assessments of their personality and performance, over this period. This study found that managers' careers could be predicted with extraordinary success from the measures used to assess them early on in their careers. However, they also found considerable evidence of the development of personality usually related to early successful experiences in their careers. Despite the fact that there has been no similar study carried out for scientists, it is reasonable to suggest that scientific careers will also develop depending on the nature of the organisational experiences they have early in their careers. As with managers, the experience with their first boss is likely to be a definitive one. Although this is not written up in scientific literature, much anecdotal evidence exists of scientists finding themselves in noxious laboratory situations. Indeed, the situation of Rosalind Franklin in Randall's laboratory, as described by Watson (1968), is probably a good example. She was a talented scientist, whose colleague Wilkins was apparently ill at ease with her. It is difficult to avoid concluding that had she been a talented man, or had she found herself with a more supportive supervisor, she might have had the encouragement and support needed to arrive earlier at the structure of DNA. Instead, Watson and Crick were allowed a preview of her work, and realised its significance immediately.

Many more mundane examples routinely occur. Scientists enter laboratories, to discover that they are underfunded, that excessive teaching loads are required, that their colleagues are undistinguished and that narrow objectives are created for them. Unfortunately, this laboratory situation is usually the norm and is more likely to stifle creative work, rather than encourage it. Contrast that with the lucky experiences of the few who join a well-funded laboratory, with excellent support of all kinds — technical, bibliographic and computational. Among the staff, this laboratory also has many of the most distinguished scientists in the world. Little if any teaching is required, and the young scientist finds himself or herself encouraged in his or her early attempts at creative problem-finding or -solving. This is the situation in most of the laboratories in which the Nobel laureates in this study are located. Herschbach in Harvard is surrounded by many of the world figures in chemistry, including Nobel prize winners, William Lipscomb, Elias James Corey and Robert Burns Woodward.

In Prelog's chemistry department in the ETH Zurich there has not been a head of the department who was not a Nobel laureate! Hewish is of the view that in applying for funding for his major long-wave radio telescope, the fact that he was located in the Cavendish Laboratory in Cambridge must have made favourable funding decisions by the Science Council more likely.

An influence on science research as important as this needs to be carefully assessed. One way of doing this is to measure climate variables using standardised instruments. Amabile and Griskievicz (1989) have developed scales to measure perceptions of the environment of work, in such a way as to assess the stimulants and obstacles to creativity. Their 'work environment inventory' 'focuses on factors in the work environment that are most likely to influence the expression and development of creative ideas'. This 135 item questionnaire measures such factors as: freedom, challenge, resources, supervisor, coworkers and recognition. The WEI scales appear to have good reliability and moderate validity, and promise to be useful in measuring the factors influencing creativity. Whether they measure factors influencing discovery or not is quite another matter, and one that it would be useful to explore. It may seem reasonable to suggest that discovery would be related to creativity, but we have little concrete evidence of any such relationship. For example, discovery may be related to resource provision or to persistence or to specific motivation more than to creativity.

Group membership and supervision

In research groups certain people have defined roles. The project leader is the person who is expected by the other members to have a wide overview of the field and a clear vision of the problem (in industry, this is referred to as 'helicopter vision'). The project leader will select people to assist on the project and will expect them to be able to explore mysterious areas of the literature and carry out exploratory experimentation, directed towards the solution of problems involved in the project. The research assistant, often someone who is also completing doctoral work, works under the supervision of the project leader, and is usually allocated responsibility for certain aspects of the work.

Lorenz (1977) has studied the effects of personal, social and sociocultural factors on the ability of scientists to develop hypotheses. He identifies mentoring, co-authoring, adversaries and colleagues as sources of ideas in relation to hypotheses. He also draws attention to the impact of ideas current in the wider society at a given time as also contributing to the nature of the hypotheses developed. He does not draw out the organisational factors which may also be important, but he does draw attention to the possibility that scientist's ability to generate hypotheses may be improved by teaching, including the teaching of the use of analogies and imaging.

Two distinct roles are discernible here. The function of the leader requires the project leader to be able to motivate and enthuse people towards their work, while that of the research assistant requires the person to be able to work well under supervision. Of course, these roles are caricatures in a way, in that few people fit precisely into these definitions. However, the basic paradigm is one of collaboration and communication. Herbert Brown puts it succinctly:

> You must have capable people working with you who are willing to listen to you and follow the work further on down.

Autonomous work groups/self-directed work teams

One of the most popular approaches to work organisation since the 1970s has been to use autonomous work groups or self-directed work teams. This is a way of organising work in which the work group has responsibility for the whole activity cycle and has the right to decide on issues connected with these activities. Such issues include who joins the group, who leads the group, the division of labour, and the method and the pace of the work. The focus here is on the group as opposed to the individual, though the group will probably have an elected or appointed leader. Many studies have shown that autonomous work groups have the advantage of benefiting the workers without sacrificing productivity. Nowadays, the reorganisation of work is often treated as just one component in the process of planned organisational change.

Autonomous groups differ from other techniques such as job rotation, job enlargement and job enrichment because they are more than just restructuring schemes. Decisions that effect the group are made by the group to a greater extent. In addition, research in the area is much more thorough than the former techniques and it is widely accepted as having a greater effect on the 'quality of working life' (QWL) movement. Dale and Cooper (1992) mention two interesting examples from industry in which autonomous work groups have had favourable effects on both productivity and morale. The first example came from the black and white television factory at Philips in the 1970s. In one of a series of studies, Den Hertog (1974) reported that when autonomous work groups were introduced, the evaluation programme revealed:

(a) lower absenteeism,
(b) lower waiting time for materials,
(c) better co-ordination and training within the groups,
(d) a 10% reduction in component costs,
(e) greater job satisfaction.

At the Olivetti plant in Italy, the long assembly line was abolished in favour of 'integrated assembly units' or 'assembly islands' (Butera, 1975). These units consisted of groups of 30 people who were responsible for assembling, inspecting and maintaining the whole product. All of the required output was produced by a number of these identical, integrated units. Butera (1975) observed the following changes:

(a) significant improvements in the quality of the product and lower wastage,
(b) an increase in the speed of product throughput and a decrease in 'in-process' time to less than a third of the assembly line system,
(c) an increase in job satisfaction and motivation,
(d) greater flexibility in allocating human resources,
(e) an increase in training costs and per capita costs.

With the exception of the increase in training and per capita costs, it seems clear from these examples that the effects on the individual and the organisation of introducing autonomous work groups are largely positive. However, one must also be aware that we may only hear about interventions that are successful. Others are unlikely to be considered of interest and are unlikely to be published.

In the industrial context, the organisation must consider the fears of middle management and first line supervisors. Autonomous groups involve a redefinition of roles within the organisation, which some may interpret as a loss of power (Dale and Cooper, 1992). Another obstacle is the necessary increase in expenditure in the initial stages of introduction. Under this system, individuals must receive comprehensive training, and in most cases will have to be paid more to reflect an increase in responsibility.

Much of the same can be said of self-directed work teams. These are functional groups of employees who manage particular production units. The work team consists of individuals trained in the necessary technical skills and who have the abilities necessary to complete specific tasks. In this way they correspond very closely to science research teams, although the connection between the design of research teams and of self-directed work teams does not seem to have been made.

Three characteristics of self-directed work teams are *semi*-autonomy (because they must report to someone), multiple skills and shared leadership. The group performs not only tasks but also plans, implements, controls and improves. Like autonomous work groups, members also take on the responsibility for selection, assessment and training and development, work pace, work methods and so on. These responsibilities are set out clearly in advance. Hence, the two terms operate under much the same principles. For the purposes of the present study, it would be useful to investigate how they might be applied to science research.

Witt (1992) argues that organisational interventions designed to reduce alienation among research scientists may have potential for success in terms of productivity. It seems logical to suggest that alienation could be reduced by manipulating existing structures or research groups, to make them more group oriented. Scientific research teams usually have some sort of hierarchical structure and contain an intellectual leader who provides creative direction (Cohen, Kruse and Anbar 1982). In previous chapters it was noted that these groups are usually small, with a principal investigator and one or more junior researchers. While it is probably necessary to have a leader (depending on the competence of each group member), research findings from autonomous work groups implies that the organisation should not interfere with the research group. Such interference could include administrative concerns, imposing the wider organisation's selection practices and introducing other constraints such as limitations of time and resources. Cohen, Kruse and Anbar (1982) distinguish between four types of group structures in scientific research which are in existence at present:

(a) highly centralised structures in which there is one authority figure and one or more subordinates,
(b) participatory structures in which core members of the team participate in the planning and executing of research tasks,
(c) highly decentralised structures, in which each individual has a subproject and there is little or no supervision and co-ordination of work in the group,

(d) participatory structures involving a concern for both administrative matters and intellectual concerns.

They concluded that much more research was needed to examine the effect of the structure of the research group on the success of that group, and also the criteria for this success. This comes as no surprise. Indeed, the need for more research is a common theme throughout this book. Taking the available evidence from industry, however, it seems reasonable to assume that turning scientific research groups into autonomous work groups could have a positive effect on performance. This is especially true given the views expressed by the scientists in the present study concerning freedom. The increase in performance, however, will most likely manifest itself in terms of quality and not quantity. The organisation should learn to see the difference.

Styles of leadership

The style of leadership used differs enormously from one project leader to another. One young biochemist went to work in a very prestigious science research institution and discovered that his project leader was very autocratic, and obsessively concerned about project deadlines and achieving goals. He found the experience of working in that laboratory so restrictive that he left after six months. He felt that the project leader was so concerned about results that he had become obsessed with the notion of results of any kind as distinct from real scientific progress. In this case, due to inexperience on the part of the supervisor, the project lost a valuable researcher, because the project leader's notion of supervision was not an appropriate one for science research. This is always a difficult judgement call for any supervisor, because he or she will wish to see results in the project of some kind within a certain period. The supervisor's judgement is important in two main areas: the first is the assessment of what constitutes progress; the second is the question of how long is an acceptable time period. Of the two the first is by far the most difficult to judge, and this is why the supervisor must adopt a 'hands on' approach. An inexperienced or unimaginative supervisor may look for precise definable progress within a relatively short period. If the emphasis is exclusively on this kind of progress, then important more valuable insights which develop along the way may be lost. Very little scientific research travels on predictable tramlines. Scientists need the freedom to explore areas that excite them, even if connections with the immediate project are difficult to see or are non-existent. A good supervisor must be able to distinguish between the talented researcher, exploring remotely associated areas which may or may not turn out to be useful in relation to the project, and another researcher who is simply wasting time. It would be a mistake to underestimate the difficulty experienced by supervisors in this respect.

It may be that it is better to organise projects in a collaborative way rather than leave all this to the supervisor. It may well be more appropriate to use discussion methods coupled with periodic presentations. Presentations have the advantage of creating deadlines. Deadlines have the advantage of focusing the mind, and group presentations mean that all those involved in a project get to know what everyone else knows. They can also offer useful suggestions to one another. Such group discussions are also a useful mechanism for identifying time-wasting activities on the part of certain members, which an individual supervisor might have difficulty with. In the work of knowledge organisations such as research laboratories a collaborative rather than a dictatorial climate is considered to be more conducive to the generation of ideas and inputs to the research process. Hurley (1990) has shown that in work involving high levels of technology, there exists a 'collaborative imperative' which obliges such organisations to so structure their work situation (by way of short hierarchies for example) that collaboration is a normal experience at work. Simonton (1988b) has studied the biographical and historical facts relating to over 2000 scientists, in order to identify social factors that might influence their creativity. He points to the fact that:

> ...most Nobel prize winners have studied under previous Nobel prize winners, or they have people around they can use for inspiration.

His research has also shown that those scientists:

> ...in networks with other scientific creators have longer and more productive careers than those who are isolated.

Simonton deduces from these findings that the role of mentors and inspired and talented colleagues is critical to the creativity of the scientist. Though scientists in general are a gregarious group of people, not every scientist finds it easy to work as part of a team or to supervise others. Frederick Sanger liked working with people:

> It always pays to have people to discuss your valuable thoughts with. I have always trusted people I have worked with.

But Heinrich Rohrer was very conscious of the possibility of a supervisor having an adverse effect on creative work:

> I simply would like to focus attention more on the fact that we probably much more easily destroy creativity, and do this much more than we foster it. I believe we should watch more what we are doing in destroying creativity, than we need to consider ways of promoting it.

Albert Einstein was of a similar opinion to Rohrer:

It is, in fact, nothing short of a miracle that the modern methods of instruction have not yet entirely strangled the holy curiosity of inquiry; for this delicate plant, aside from stimulation, stands mostly in need of freedom; without this it goes to wreck and ruin without fail. It is a very grave mistake to think that the enjoyment of seeing and searching can be promoted by means of coercion and a sense of duty (Schlipp, 1951, p. 17).

In one of the very few studies of group effects on scientific creativity (though not on discovery), Andrews (1975) identified four social psychological factors that influenced creativity. These were:

(a) high responsibility for initiating new activities,
(b) high degree of power to hire research assistants,
(c) no interference from an administrative superior,
(d) high stability of employment.

The contrast between the way in which creative scientist work best and the organisation of those involved in routine work is very striking. The organisation that can best facilitate the creative scientist provides the above conditions.

Most of the literature on organisation derives from studies of large organisations such as the army, the church, the industrial plant and bureaucratic institutions such as government agencies. Hence, many of the theoretical bases for the training of managers and CEOs derive from organisations that are inappropriate for creative scientific research. There can therefore be significant losses to creative research due to attempts to mould scientists to a management model more suitable for an accounts department or a production plant. Very little has been studied specifically in relation to science research groups, and so little is known about the precise role of the group in encouraging creativity in research (Amabile, 1983).

Some social psychologists, notably Andrews and Gordon (1970), Pelz and Andrews (1976) and Amabile (1983), have done valuable work in this area, and Amabile (1983), as we have seen in Chapter 2, has produced a model of the organisational processes of creativity. This model presents the sequences proposed for creative processes and their accompanying individual characteristics. Though developed in a social environment in industry, this is a model that may well have useful application in studying discovery in science research.

Organisation culture

The principal investigator in a research project can influence the organisational culture to a very great extent. Many aspects of that culture have nothing whatever to do with the resources, but reflect the particular personality of the principal investigator, and the culture he or she establishes within the research group. In a recent review of the literature, Boxenbaum (1991) found that many studies have shown that, for scientists, the following organisational cultures promote creative research:

(a) an atmosphere of psychological safety, one that emphasises encouragement, understanding, freedom of thought;
(b) a culture where creativity and innovation are the norm;
(c) one where attempts are not made to turn talented researchers into mediocre managers;
(d) one which has the necessary resources.

On the other hand, he found that the following organisational characteristics are likely to stifle individual creativity:

(a) a military or command-mode structure,
(b) undue organisational caution,
(c) a 'don't rock the boat' mentality,
(d) an overemphasis on extrinsic (institutional) motivation.

We can see that this is supportive of the Andrews (1975) study cited earlier in this chapter. Boxenbaum also makes the point that the goals of a research project should not be written in stone. Too often, the research supervisor is reluctant to set off in new directions because of his or her concerns about deadlines. It is the larger organisation that causes these concerns by focusing on administrative matters. Implicit in the descriptions of discovery by the scientists in this study (and in many others) is that the scientists were very good managers and organisers. Insights that they had (perhaps as some accident of upbringing or acquaintance) were useful to them in organising their scientific research. These skills and insights remain obscure and implicit. Because it is not their domain, scientists are often reluctant, lacked the motivation or were ill-equipped with the vocabulary to make explicit the organisational and managerial strategies they used in their science. However, there is no reason why scientists should not use available skills and techniques from whatever field, if it can be useful in the pursuit of discovery. Collaborative or authoritarian research group climate, ideas, knowledge and techniques are the main inputs to the research process: failure is its most usual outcome. This frequent failure is well known to experienced scientists, and it requires a particular kind of perseverance to continue to work enthusiastically in the face of repeated negative results. For most scientists, this makes the group setting of their research a most important variable. The group can provide badly needed social support when experiments are failing, and can be a powerful source of ideas in relation to the solution of difficult problems of a theoretical, experimental or technical nature. Blumberg tells us:

I have always found science a very social occupation, an awful lot of interaction takes place between scientists. It is the exact opposite to the image of the lone scientist...yes, we went to meetings, but most of the time we sat around and talked to each other—sometimes trivial gossip, but mostly scientific discussions. There are tremendous communication possibilities in modern science.

The experience of working in research at its best is characterised by the excitement of approaching nature's secrets. In an exciting, creative laboratory, where discovery is taking place, the group experiences appear to support this. Rohrer, speaking about his work at the ETH Zurich, describes the development of a good spirit in the laboratory as follows:

A spirit evolved in the research laboratory, and Olsen (their research supervisor) was clever enough to recognise it, and to simply leave it alone. I think spirits are usually created too by the participants; if you simply offer the right environment, the participants can make the spirit. The crucial thing is for the supervisor to notice this spirit and take care that it is not destroyed. We had seminars; just a few guys together with two other guys; we called them our 'Idioten Colloquium' (Seminar of the Idiots). That is where we simply did a few things—not very high brow things. It was very simple but nevertheless we got together and talked about certain things of interest to us, everybody had to give 1, 2 or 3 seminars maybe over a month on a certain topic. It was a very casual group, really a group of friends, so it never was a matter to show the other guys how clever you are. We had a very good relationship, and sure you did not want to appear a fool when it was your time to present, and when it was the other guy's time, you had to learn too.

This is a very human description of the development of a research group which had a good group dynamic. It was a group in which people were helped to develop and progress their own thinking, but using the group as an intelligent sounding-board for new ideas. Anthony Hewish describes the Cavendish Laboratory approach in similar terms:

We had group seminars once a week, where we tore the published literature to pieces. We looked upon the rest of the world with some disdain; we thought we were the best group in the world. We did, however, overlook certain developments. For example, important discoveries were being made in Russia at that time but we did not have a Russian translator so we missed out on that. Apart from that, we felt that we were on top of the literature. Of course there was not as much published in those days.

These accounts suggest that our Nobel laureates found the group experience essentially a rewarding one. It may also have helped them in their development and towards their discoveries. Certainly, the scientists in these interviews strongly supported the importance of the group to them. Yet surprisingly little research has been carried out into this important area. This may be a case where the myth and stereotype of the lone creative genius secluded in his laboratory obscures the interactive reality of present-day scientific research. Fortunately, it is also an area where those responsible for the management and organisation of research projects are in a position to define their own policies. Those policies and practices could be aimed at avoiding leaving these positive experiences to chance (which the scientists in this study were lucky enough to experience). A number of important facts and insights are known about effective science research groups, which have important implications for the processes that take place in a research group. One of the most comprehensive studies of scientists in their organisations was carried out by Pelz and Andrews from 1951 to 1965, and reported in 1976. This very thorough study, for the first time approached the scientist as a member of a group, and of a wider organisation. Pelz and Andrews' work was useful in studying the actual work scientists do. In Chapter 13, p. 260, for example, they discuss the results of their study as showing the delicate relationship that exists between the creative scientist's freedom and the relationships within the group and with the supervisor. They conclude: the supervisor 'is a neutral sounding board; he draws out their ideas'. Clearly, the organisational environment has an effect on individual scientists. In an interview carried out for this study, Frederick Sanger said: 'One works well with people one likes.' Many scientists believe, with Sanger, that science research is a very social affair and depends quite considerably on interpersonal relationships to help the creative process forward. However, most scientists would also agree with Ernst that the main source of ideas is within themselves. According to Ernst: 'I never knew a team create an idea.'

These often paradoxical ideas illustrate the intricate nature of the research process. The reality of the role of the creative scientist is that he or she must work in an increasingly complex laboratory and is, by necessity, part of a research team. The scientist needs to be aware of what other people are doing and be able to discuss their ideas with others. Nevertheless, it is within their own minds that something new develops. It is therefore of considerable interest to scientists to know what group activities and processes take place in groups which encourage the creative individual to be creative. Of course, it is also useful to know what aspects of the group experience can discourage this creativity, so that these can be avoided. The scientists in the present study attached great importance to their own minds as the primary source of their ideas. However, they also attached considerable importance to the role their colleagues played in stimulating those ideas. In the present study Ernst tells us:

> I think, ideally, you need to be courageous to try new ideas; yet not too self-confident that you think you are always right and can't accept new ideas.

Blumberg's research was significantly assisted by group work:

> We set aside a 1 or 2 hour session every week to come together and build on each other's ideas. We tried to make it ego-free where you would come forward with an idea but not identify it with yourself. Someone would present a body of data and we would come up with ideas. We would end up with a formulation for a study design.

Table 11 Productivity and average ranking of idea sources abbreviated from Glueck and Jauch, 1975

Source of ideas	Mean scores	Rank of means
Professors in department	4.08	4
Non-departmental colleagues	4.64	5
Colleagues not in university	3.26	3
Own previous work	1.68	1
Literature on subject	2.29	2
Client or sponsor	5.01	6

This is a fascinating description of the collegial nature of the group work involved in modern science. Glueck and Jauch (1975) carried out a study among 160 research scientists working in a variety of departments. Their study explored the source of scientists' main research ideas. Table 11 gives these results.

The rank-ordered results show that scientists saw themselves as the main source of their ideas, closely followed by the literature on the subject. Interestingly, colleagues not in their own laboratory were a strong third in importance, followed by professors in their own department. These findings support similar findings in the Pelz and Andrews study on the effect of valued colleagues on the generation of ideas. It is clear from these studies, and from the present one, that scientists are quite unlike administrative people in their need for social support from colleagues. They operate as uniquely talented individuals with a very powerful internal source of ideas.

Communications in research groups

Research collaboration depends greatly on good communications. The principal investigator establishes systems (such as Rohrer's 'Idioten Colloquium') with the purpose of ensuring good communication of ideas within the group. Scientists need to review the literature, design their experiments, in an atmosphere where they know they can call on their colleagues for help, advice or to explore some puzzling aspect of the research they are involved in. Information flow is central to good science; if aspects of what is known are suppressed, hidden or not available to all the scientists working in a particular area, then progress can be seriously impeded. The 'invisible college' which Polanyi considers so important to international progress in science cannot exist without full and open information flow. Hence, access to the most effective information retrieval systems is essential, as is the ability to attend related conferences. Electronic mail now provides a wonderfully open system of communication between scientists. Computer-assisted bibliographic searching and CD-ROMS provide high levels of access to existing research, but of course

Table 12   Increase in potential relationships with increase in group size

Size of group	Number of relationships
2	1
3	6
4	25
5	90
6	301
7	966

it has to be published before it can be retrieved. Communication within the research group is essential. Hewish says:

> I think the most damaging thing you could do in organising your group would be simply not to talk to anyone — no communication. Just give them their project and say: 'Come back to me in a month's time and let me know how you are getting on.'

This approach would be seen as dismissive, and discourage regular communication. The organisational implication of this in terms of budgetary support, library facilities and staff development systems is fairly clear.

Size of research groups

The predominant finding in relation to size of a group in organisations in general has been that small groups tend to function better than large ones. Small groups tend to have better communications, members tend to get on with one another better and they are more productive. Therefore, another responsibility of the principal investigator is to hold the size of the group down or, if it has to grow large, to appoint more principal investigators. This is probably related to the complexity of possible relationships that can exist — the larger the group the greater the complexity. Kephart (1950) has shown the influence of group size on possible relationships (see Table 12).

Apart from communication becoming more complex and relationships increasing, it is also possible that the levels of trust and intimacy, and sharing of ideas, will diminish as the research group becomes larger. Shaw (1989) has shown that the perceived distance between the leader and the rest of the group increases, the larger the group. Larger groups tend to become more structured, more rule based, more hierarchical and less flexible. Science groups are in a favourable position, since most research groups are very small indeed (usually ranging in size from two to six people).

The reward system in research

Rewards can also be used to encourage creative science. If people are rewarded for innovation, for publishing exciting and perhaps controversial articles, then creative science is more likely to occur than if they are rewarded for simply completing a project on time or for satisfactorily finishing their doctoral work. This is a matter that is most frequently left to traditional practice. However, it is an area where new institutional policies can define those outcomes that will be rewarded and encouraged. Not all science research groups have happy and fruitful experiences. Leopold (1978) has pointed out that the increasing complexity of modern science requiring expensive equipment and extensive technical assistance has resulted in 'bureaucratic science'. This makes the individual scientist increasingly dependent on two interacting factors: (a) government granting agencies, foundations or business interests as sources of funds and (b) the scientific establishment, which through peer evaluation determines who does what in research. This factor determines placements in better jobs, allocates access to the more prestigious publications and advises grant agencies as to which research projects should be funded. Thus, according to Leopold, the reward system of science determines the extent to which an individual scientist can be creative. He hypothesises:

> The bureaucratization of science will cause personal and political factors to interfere increasingly with creativity.

If this were to occur as a matter of general practice it could of course be very damaging for science.

Group duration effects

Groups tend to experience reductions in productivity after some years. Wells and Pelz (1976) suggest that for creative problem solving to be effective, groups 'should not to think alike, nor be sure how other members would approach a new problem.' (Pelz and Andrews, 1976, p. 241). As groups stay together for long periods, they tend to develop 'groupthink' (Janis, 1982) — a way of thinking alike which can be quite diminishing of any individual freedom to think differently. In their study, Pelz and Andrews (1976) found that scientists' average scientific contribution was greatest in the period when their group was under five years old. After that, a fairly sharp decline took place. They also found that research groups declined in frequency of communications and in cohesiveness over a similar period. Andrews (1967) refers to the 'payoff from creative ability' and argues that the following factors influence the research group:

(a) time in the particular area,
(b) time on a particular project,
(c) degree of co-ordination in the group,
(d) communication in the group.

Although Andrews dealt more with the production of creative ideas than productivity in general, both factors appear to be influenced by group duration effects. Generally speaking, science groups do not last very long. In university research, the groups exist either for the completion of a doctoral project, which usually does not last longer than five years, or they exist to carry out specific funded research projects, which also have a predetermined life-span. However, if the groups are more time stable, as, for example, in the research laboratory of a commercial organisation, then regular changes in the composition of the research groups are likely to improve the group performance. Wells and Pelz (1976) showed, for example, that groups declined in performance after several years in existence. The implications of this finding could include the fact that research teams should as a matter of regular practice be re-formed after a few years in existence, in order to stimulate more creative work. Based on the research available, the fact that most research groups are small in size and do not last very long augers well in terms of group effectiveness. However, they are not the only influential factors. Other examples include: collaborative versus authoritarian control systems, involvement with highly effective scientists, the reward system, communication within the group and group creativity development.

One review by Bland and Ruffin (1992) covered studies from 1960 to 1990 and found a set of characteristics which in their assessment were consistently related to research productivity. They were:

(a) clear goals that serve as coordinating mechanisms,
(b) research emphasis,
(c) distinctive culture,
(d) positive group climate,
(e) assertive participative governance,
(f) decentralised organisation,
(g) frequent communication,
(h) accessible resources, particularly human ones,
(i) sufficient size, age and diversity in the research group,
(j) appropriate rewards,
(k) concentration on recruitment and selection,
(l) leadership with research expertise and skill in both initiating appropriate organisational structure,
(m) using participatory management practices.

Ekvall and Tangeberg-Andersson (1986) also found that the climate of a creative research laboratory is characterised by high levels of challenge, freedom, dynamism, idea-support and trust. A number of these factors are now explored further.

4 CAPITALISING ON CHANCE

We have seen in Chapter 5 that chance is a phenomenon that discoverer-scientists are able to capitalise on. Organisationally, it might be possible to increase the likelihood of scientists making use of the inevitable chance occurrences that pervade research. Some techniques that have been used in this respect are outlined here.

Brainstorming

Within any group, dynamics of different kinds emerge. In science, most groups predictably, approach the solution of science problems in an entirely rational way. Science research explores a very minute area of the natural world in great depth. Many research groups find that sometimes by exploring the topic in this way, progress slows down and ideas around the problem seems to become sterile and unproductive. This is a well-known psychological phenomenon, which has been recognised by the development of a number of group problem-solving techniques, which use both rational and intuitive approaches to problems. Included in this group is the technique of brainstorming. Brainstorming is a technique of creative problem-solving which separates the process of idea generation from the process of evaluation. The evaluation of ideas is known to diminish the flow of ideas. The idea in brainstorming is to get the quantity of ideas first, because among this larger quantity some useful germs of good ideas may exist. The evaluation of these ideas is then carried out. The development of the ideas is a further phase in the technique of brainstorming. The usefulness of brainstorming can be demonstrated in the famous exercise: 'uses of the brick'. If a group is asked to think of as many uses as they can for a common object, such as a brick, they often think of large numbers of uses very quickly. After a while the production of ideas diminishes and eventually ends. If at that stage or when the idea generation slows down, a diversion is created, such as each member speaking about their private interests, idea production will improve again. After a diversion of perhaps ten minutes, it is found that many more uses for the brick are rapidly found (see Figure 9).

Perhaps the most important aspect of this process is that the group develops many more ideas than individuals working on their own. What are the reasons for this? It would seem to be related to the increased variety of associative cues which the diversion has provided, thus allowing new ideas on the topic to be produced. After the brainstorming exercise has been completed, certain ideas must be filtered out due to concerns such as cost, availability of resources, time and practicality. Of course, the number of constraints are dictated by the organisation, and it is important that potentially exciting ideas are not ruled out by an overemphasis on time and cost. Wherever possible, the decision should be made by the research group.

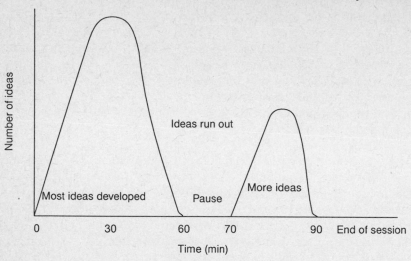

Figure 9   The 'pause' effect in brainstorming

Synectics

This technique of creative problem-solving has been developed further in the system known as 'synectics'. The synectics method employs a number of additional techniques for the encouragement of new ideas. Brainstorming techniques are used to begin with and then, in a separate session, the ideas are not evaluated but put in the form of possible uses. Each idea is initially regarded as having some possible merit. Then the disadvantages of each idea are turned into positives by imagining how the disadvantages could be overcome. I have seen this technique used in the development of research ideas very successfully, when the research group found itself running out of useful ideas for further progress. According to Prince (1980), who developed synectics, the six cognitive processes that take place in idea generation are: wishing, retrieving, imaging, comparing, transformation and storing. In 'wishing' we are motivated to have a new idea. The rivalry for attention that usually exists in a group, but not on one's own, can increase this motivation. In 'retrieving' we collect information from the memory which might be useful in the generation of this new idea or in the solution of this particular problem. 'Imaging' involves developing mental pictures of possible solutions, comparing these ideas with existing ones, transforming them where necessary and storing the idea. According to Prince, this process of idea generation is greatly inhibited by other learned cognitive processes. For example, our general habit of having criteria to evaluate our own performance tends to diminish our creative capacity. Furthermore, our habits of social thinking, developed in

Table 13 Characteristics of routine and speculative thinking

Characteristics of routine thinking	Characteristics of creative thinking
1. Logical	1. You do not know where you are going
2. Empirical	2. You do not know how you are going to get there
3. Few mistakes tolerated	3. Focus is on the process as well as the result
4. Focus on task completion	4. Many mistakes are necessary
5. Predictable	5. Much confusion
6. Comfortable	6. Much uncertainty
7. Low risk	7. High risk
8. Socially acceptable	8. Not provable in advance
9. Supported	9. Makes you anxious, unpredictable, appears inefficient and wasteful, easy to reject as impractical or impossible

order to help us get on with others, interfere with our uniquely individual approach to ideas. In Table 13 Prince (1970) lists a number of characteristics of both routine and speculative thinking to illustrate our frequent reluctance to be speculative.

This table reminds us of the range of powerful forces ranged against truly novel ways of looking at things, important in the development of new ideas. These forces exist in our own minds — the enemy within — and may be reenforced or diminished by group or supervisory approaches to them. This table also helps us understand why it is that the truly creative individual has to be free in order to be creative — free of damaging societal or group pressures and free to think in new ways without being constrained by attachment to existing paradigms. Such characteristics exist in some few people, some of whom are artistically, some scientifically oriented. Even fewer of this subgroup will be comprehensively educated and trained in a scientific discipline. The table illustrates the difficulty inherent in moving into the truly speculative area of ideas, when compared to the more predictable and less risky option of routine thinking. Of course there is an irony in all of this. The more routine the thinking the less creative will be the research, and hence the whole project, and the reputations of those involved, will be at risk. Conversely, the more speculative and creative (and therefore riskier) the project, the more it is likely to succeed in developing some new insight in science, and enhancing the reputation of those involved! This is lateral thinking. De Bono (1971) favours rather similar processes in order to stimulate his 'lateral thinking' — a mode of thinking most probably associated with creativity. He points out that for effective brainstorming sessions to work, they need the cross-stimulation of other members of a group. In other words, the creative process in science is likely to be helped considerably by working in a stimulating research group, rather than entirely on one's own. He also believes that analogies are useful in the creative process and that group dynamics can develop the ability to draw analogies, and bring them in from a wide variety of sources.

Serendipity

Serendipity is much cited as a source of discovery. Serendipity is that phenomenon where a scientist stumbles into a discovery, when actually looking into something else. According to Kantorovich and Ne'eman (1989), scientists usually work within the parameters of existing science. If they were to remain in this state forever the existing paradigm science would remain 'normal' or unexceptional. Serendipity allows them blind variations, which in some cases may help turn the existing world-view on its head. Serendipity is a well-known phenomenon, but singularly little used! We teach science as normal science, following the scientific method, using logic and existing techniques. Science is usually taught also as a monolithic collection of insights, not as a gradual process of the development of new insights. The disadvantage of this is that many young scientists expect logic alone to provide them with discoveries of consequence; they are frequently disappointed. The testing of hypotheses is outlined at great length in many texts; the development of hypotheses is not discussed. The processes by which discoveries are made remain a mystery. Lenox (1985) makes the point that:

> Many authors present their results in such a way that one is led to believe that the entire project was logically obvious from the start, and that the author only collected data to verify his hypothesis. Presenting material to the scientific community in such a way that the actual processes of discovery is omitted or hidden from colleagues has been termed 'retrospective falsification'. While a scientist may be unwilling or even embarrassed to admit that his or her results are perhaps the work of chance discovery, he or she does a disservice to the scientific community at large and to students in particular by not sharing a true example of the discovery process.

Here is an opportunity for the science research group to learn these processes, not to leave their occurrence to remote chance. Lenox (1985) describes three methods by which scientists are led to discovery: the Aufbau or building-up method, the method of insight and the method of chance or serendipitous discovery. In order to educate the scientist for serendipity, Lenox suggest a number of methods (in addition to rigorous training in science, of course). They are:

(a) In order to develop imaginative solutions from minimal information the hidden object exercise can be used; an object such as a clothes-peg is placed in a box which is sealed and students are asked to identify it. Does it roll? Does it have corners? Does it slide smoothly? This forces the student to devise novel methods of gathering data and to interpret imaginatively. The methods of observation and recording can be honed by this method.

(b) The exposure of young scientists to long-term projects rather than small individual experiments gives them a true picture of the scale of scientific research and the amount of time and rigorous recording needed.
(c) The development of flexibility of thought, without having the thought processes becoming rigidly fixed. Careful consideration of all results, even apparently unsuccessful ones, can be a useful flexibility developing experience. Lenox puts it like this: 'Students are rarely able to say anything about the actual results except that they did not see what they expected to see. No true observations have been made, and little or no contemplation of the experiment has taken place.'
(d) Rigorous preparation before attempting to investigate a problem.
(e) Modelling avid curiosity.

Lenox tells us:

...there is no doubt that the curiosity of one person and his enthusiasm for discovery have a pronounced effect on others...a good teacher of science should be the very model of insatiable scientific curiosity.

The foregoing attempts to give the reasons why a research group—as a group—is important to science. The scientific research group can either be characterised as open and creative, and encourage such forms of thinking and problem-solving, or it can develop 'groupthink', where conformity to existing norms is closely adhered to. The development of that research group is therefore of critical importance to the development of science. Brainstorming and 'synectics' are very useful tools in the development of idea generation in the research group. Instead of leaving the development of the group as a problem-solving entity to chance, it is taken under the control of the group or the research supervisor. The production of new and creative ideas is seen as something that may be encouraged or developed, and not as an intervention of 'magical' chance. The active pursuit of serendipitous lines of research as described by Lenox might be more fruitful than leaving serendipity entirely to chance!

Of course, we do not want to attribute more than is justifiable to serendipity. It is common to attach considerable importance to it, and that may be reasonable. Roberts (1989) gives many examples of serendipitous effects in scientific discovery, but, as he points out, much is also attributable to the sagacity of the scientist who trips serendipitously into something of interest. Root-Bernstein (1988) has also revisited many discoveries attributed to chance, and a careful re-examination of these shows that the preparedness and the persistence of the scientist were the primary factors in reaching the discovery (see Chapter 5).

Innovation and discovery

Innovation is a term used in a variety of ways, with little agreement on its precise meaning. Nevertheless, we can learn from the innovation literature much of what can be done — at the level of the organisation — to stimulate new ways of thinking. Most writers construe innovation to mean innovation in organisations, whether this be new systems, technologies or processes (Damanpour, 1987).

Typical of this view of innovation is Damanpour's view that there are two main typologies of innovation: technological innovation, and administrative innovation. Damanpour (1987) describes technological innovations as those that:

> ...occur as a result of the use of a new tool, technique, device, or system. They produce changes in products or services, or in the way those products are produced, or those services are rendered...Administrative innovations are those that change an organisation's structure or its administrative processes.

This view of innovation as changes in the organisation itself, as distinct from its outputs, is the most dominant one in the literature (see West and Farr, 1990). Indeed, though this is the dominant preoccupation in the literature, it is often widely assumed that innovation is the same as creativity, and even discovery. However, as we have seen above in this chapter, creativity is a capacity of the personality which may or may not have any relationship with discovery. Furthermore, innovation has as its main object the organisation itself, not the production of new ideas or products as in the case of discovery.

Rosenfeld and Servo (1990) take a startlingly different view. They state that:

$$\text{Innovation} = \text{conception} + \text{invention} + \text{exploitation}$$

which appears to include the whole process of discovery. It seems unlikely that an organisation capable of a process so revolutionary as invention could also be so production and operations oriented that it could also exploit such developments. In Burroughs Wellcome, research is clearly separated from exploitation; though links do exist between both processes, they are not formal or strong.

Amabile (1988) focuses on innovation within organisations and models innovation in organisations as shown in Figure 10.

Though this model focuses on innovation within any organisation, it may well have some applicability to discovery within a laboratory also. This would probably be a useful guide to further research studies, focusing on discovery rather than innovation or creativity.

Findlay and Lumsden (1988) put forward an evolutionary view of creativity, which could have implications for our approach to creativity among scientists in laboratories. The model they propose is given here as Figure 11.

Though primarily a cognitive theory, this theory is one of very few among the creativity studies to take account of the wider social environment, within which most scientists work, and may well have a considerable effect on patterns of discovery.

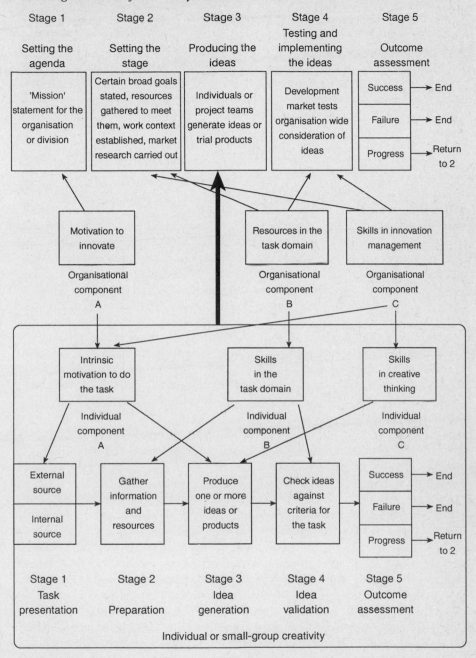

Figure 10 Componential model of organisational innovation (Reproduced with permission from Amabile, 1988)

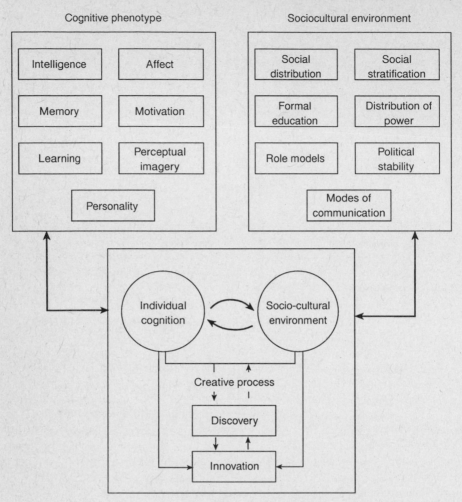

Figure 11 The Findlay and Lumsden model of the relationship between the creative process, discovery and innovation

This chapter is an attempt to show the many ways in which organisation factors may affect the individual scientist. These range from the obvious first organisational action and selection to the range of interventions that may occur depending to some extent on the leadership and sophistication of key organisational members. Of course, all this implies an organisational theory of discovery. Chapter 7 proposes an organisational model and suggests research to test it.

Chapter 7

The Discovery Zone

When this project commenced, it was seen as an exploration of the correlates of discovery in science. As this book reaches a conclusion, it is easy to see why many have steered well clear of the topic of discovery. The logical-positivists excluded it because it was non-logical; psychologists substituted creativity for it, probably because they considered creativity to be a major antecedent of discovery; social psychologists substituted scientific productivity for discovery, probably because they regarded productivity as easier to define and measure.

To exclude discovery — the apex of scientific research — or to substitute for it some other concept, seems a limited way of viewing the world of science. It is as if science is seen only as the mechanics of experimental proof; the great glory of it, when new insights emerge and are developed, is overlooked. Dissatisfied with the emphasis on experimental proof, many scientists have referred to the need for work on hypothesis development and generation, yet surprisingly little has been done on this, compared to the vast array of studies on experimental method. It is easier to understand the reluctance to use discovery as an outcome measure in favour of some other concept such as creativity or scientific productivity; discovery is very difficult to define.

1 SUMMARY OF PRECEDING CHAPTERS

In designing this project, the first difficulty encountered was in finding a definition for scientific discovery. As we have seen in the first chapter, definitions of discovery in science are very difficult to arrive at. Many discussions took place during which the author explored, with scientists, their ideas about what constitutes discovery. Their views on discovery ranged from seeing it as discontinuous (in the sense that either a discovery is made or it is not made) to seeing it as incremental.

This latter view is that science progresses by small steps and tiny advances which can amount over time to something quite substantial. This is the

Kuhnian view that science progresses as evolutionary science, in Kuhn's terms, until so many anomalies occur that a paradigm shift is needed in order to explain the facts of nature more inclusively.

Though a satisfactory definition of discovery proved to be elusive, it was decided that a study of discovery would need to be based among scientists about whom there was agreement that they were discoverers. There is substantial agreement that Nobel laureates fall into that category. However, it is also clear that many scientists who do not receive Nobel prizes, also make discoveries. For this reason, the question of what constitutes discovery, is something which scientists really need to work on, to see if an adequate and acceptable definition of discovery could be arrived at. Such a definition would need to be testable, and would avoid the pitfalls of trivialising discovery on the one hand, or being utterly exclusive on the other.

The elusiveness of discovery to definition is no coincidence, and matches the elusiveness of discovery itself. However, the substitution of other terms such as creativity or productivity to stand for discovery in some way, is also not satisfactory. Simply because we may operationalise a term more easily does not mean it is a valid substitute for the reality which eludes us.

In discussions, the Nobel laureates raised as key issues a number of points and these are listed in the Preface of this book. They referred to differing methods and approaches to scientific research, that is to say the need for differing methods of scientific experimentation, and to training in these methods; the need to be free to think and experiment. They referred to the importance of chance in research, and to the need to have the right colleagues within a research project.

Let me be quite clear; these factors were not referred to in organisational terms by the Nobel laureates. Indeed many of them referred to organisation in rather negative terms. Significantly however, they emphasised the need for substantial resources for their research; to the need for the selection of excellent colleagues; to the need for the proper preparation of young scientists; to the need for good supervision and leadership, and for good technical and other supports within the University or laboratory.

The Nobel laureates in this study see these matters as the normal requirements of scientific projects. They do not see them in organisational terms. It is my own conclusion, that there is an organisational dimension to discovery, based on reflection on my discussions with the Nobel laureates, and the topics they raised and emphasised. It is a conclusion based also on what are observed to be the facts of the situation in which these discoverer-scientists located themselves; in particular, the fact that all of them had joined at an early age, and remained with laboratories which were very substantially resourced. It is my conclusion based on these facts, that organisational ability, and resources of an organisational kind are extremely important to a scientific project. It is my view that there is a strong *implied organisational dimension* in the actual practice of scientific research, though this is rarely acknowledged.

The individual scientist is the centre of the discovery-related project, yet surprisingly little can be said with absolute certainty about the discoverer-scientist in terms of personality characteristics. In examining the creativity literature from the perspective of scientific discovery, it was seen that it contained a number of weaknesses which create difficulties for any attempt to relate creativity to discovery. The creativity of the individual scientist in generating ideas may well contribute to discovery in science. However, from the results of the present study it seems that the scientists' persistence and patience, combined with their training, and the resources, freedom and encouragement provided by the organisation, are catalytic components which allow these ideas to come to fruition. The Nobel laureates stress the importance of having colleagues of high quality and having absolute intellectual freedom in their work.

The importance of the organisational dimension of science is not to underestimate or diminish the professional skills and abilities of the individual scientist. These skills include the ability to use various scientific methods, and to be able to reflect on both the larger and the smaller aspects of the particular research. It would seem that a knowledge of the different philosophical viewpoints which underpin the development of research and experimentation, could be useful to the scientists as part of the preparation phase. Bacon, for example, pointed to the importance of observation and experimentation, that correspond to the modern ideas of hypothesis generation and experimental design. Kuhn makes the distinction between normal and revolutionary science, of which the latter (it is proposed) may be more important for discovery. And finally, Popper argued for bold predictions and subsequent attempts at falsification (as opposed to searching for confirmations.)

Science research is directly related to problem solving, but there is debate as to whether or not the discovery process purely involves problem solving, or whether other processes are involved. According to some authors, including Einstein and Infeld, *problem-finding* may be an even more important component of creativity than problem solving. The Nobel laureates in the present study, however, were extremely reluctant to describe their work as creative. Rather, they viewed it as hard work, aided by useful insights or 'smart foraging' in Perkins's (1992) terms. Kantorovich (1993) agrees with this view, arguing that discovery is open to all scientists, provided they do not kill off their capacity to discover, with excessive logical thinking. Therefore, taking the views of these authors into account, the suggestion is made that logic is a necessary but insufficient basis for discovery.

Studies have also dealt with the development of ideas and the thinking processes involved in the individual, but tend not to acknowledge the organisation in which these discoveries took place, or the financial and human resources which were available to these scientists.

We can see quite clearly from Table 4 that all of the Nobel laureates in this study, conducted their research in well-resourced institutions. They also had the opportunity to discuss problems and issues with other distinguished scientists within these institutions. The organisational ability of the principal researcher, and the complexity of the organisational dimension of their research, is described using three examples from among the Nobel laureates, in Chapter 4. The extensive resources available to them are shown in Table 4, and this is suggestive of the effect of working in a well-resourced organisation, on discovery.

There is an uneven world-wide distribution of Nobel prize winners — with most located in Europe and the United States. Within the US and Europe, prize winners come from only a few universities (and these are the well resourced ones). When one considers that natural scientific talent is likely to be distributed evenly throughout the world, these figures form an argument for the organisational point of view. Here it is suggested that an organisational framework related to discovery may be a useful one in advancing discovery.

The phrase 'organisational framework' with its connotations of constraint, command and control might strike a chill in many scientists' hearts. Yet we have here an apparent paradox: all the Nobel laureates made their discoveries working in laboratories embedded in large well-resourced organisations. In my view, no paradox is involved. It is no accident that scientific discovery should take place in well resourced organisations. Rather, it is my view that it is that such organisations are capable of facilitating the dedicated scientist in a way other organisations are not capable of doing. Part of this organisational dimension is the creation of a climate of freedom, and one in which the opportunities provided by chance can be availed of. Organisational controls which limit the freedom given to the scientist can have profound effects on his/her ability to produce creative work, and so the fruitfulness of projects may be damaged. The responses of our Nobel laureates to the 'freedom questionnaire' showed that they attach maximum importance to aspects of the questionnaire relating to their own freedom of thought, including being able to choose what to work on. This freedom has enabled these scientists to question existing frameworks, however widely accepted they may be. It is argued in this text, that if scientists who accept existing structures of science become the dominant group, it is less likely that new and important insights will be achieved. This suggests strong organisational implications for the selection, training and supervision of scientists.

Many scientists have emphasised the role of chance in their discoveries and have, with Pasteur, taken the view that 'Chance favours the prepared mind.' Yet a rather fatalistic view of chance seems also to exist, that ignores the possibility of the preparation of the scientist's mind. Examples of discovery in science illustrate that chance brings new insights only in some cases and to only a few scientists. In attributing discovery to chance, we ignore the part played by careful observation, analogous thinking and the prepared mind. This way of thinking has also led to a lack of interest in organisational research in this area, despite the possibility that good organisational support sets the scene for the scientist to capitalise on chance opportunities. In other words, trained scientists in well-organised laboratories put themselves in a position to capitalise on opportunities (accidental or otherwise) that may arise.

Organisations are often seen in negative terms by scientists, yet there are many ways by which organisations can profoundly influence discovery. Like any human construction, organisations can be used negatively or positively. Many organisational factors, including group dynamics, selection and capitalising on chance, were explored in Chapter 6. The dynamics of the particular research group can have a profound effect on the likelihood of discovery taking place. For example, the actions of the principal investigator and the wider organisation affect morale in the laboratory (anecdotal evidence and examples from industry attest to this). It is argued that the most usual laboratory situation (narrow objectives, under-funding, excessive teaching loads) has a negative effect on morale and tends to stifle creativity.

Other organisational influences on discovery are explored in this chapter, including: within-group communications; the selection of the research team; the climate within the group; the reward system; and organisational systems to help capitalise on chance.

The foregoing chapters have highlighted the possible importance of the organisation, and of organisation as an ability or skill, in relation to successful research. They also suggest the need for more research into the organisational aspects of discovery in science, and the need to focus less on the individual and more on the group. The remainder of this final chapter will be devoted to outlining the implications of this book for future research as well as the direction which this future research should take. Now at this point it seems appropriate to discuss the relationship between individual processes, organisational processes, with discovery as the outcome, and to present this in the form of a model.

2 TOWARDS AN ORGANISATIONAL MODEL OF DISCOVERY IN SCIENCE

Within the sphere of organisational life, existing data on the distribution of substantial discovery in science, suggests strongly that exceptional scientific talent in science, even coupled with high levels of creativity, is unlikely to be sufficient for scientists to discover. If such people are located in laboratories where inadequate organisational resources are at their disposal, discovery is unlikely to occur. This is not simply the familiar argument that 'more resources will lead to more discovery' rather it is an argument for more resources, *and* a more developed scientific organisation.

We cannot state with absolute certainty that discovery will only take place in those laboratories which are very well resourced. Firstly, we cannot define what is discovery in any wholly agreed or entirely satisfactory way. Secondly, we cannot be certain what constitutes a substantial level of resources. If resources meant only money, we could measure differences easily, but if we define resources to include other dimensions such as the existence of stimulating colleagues, then agreement on a measure becomes more difficult. Yet we are all aware of the importance of stimulating discourse to generate and sharpen thinking, conceptualising and experimental ideas.

On the basis of what evidence we have, it would appear that the discoverer-scientist would find himself or herself an organisation which supports, facilitates and encourages unusual and imaginative work, with all the risks of failure associated with that. The freedom and autonomy of the scientist is respected, though certain formal objectives are well understood. The discoverer-scientist finds in that organisation, other imaginative scientific minds, and the wider organisation is sufficiently small to facilitate cross-disciplinary discussion. The laboratories are staffed with well qualified scientists capable of carrying out elaborate experiments in exquisite detail. They are assisted by well-trained and highly developed technicians. The laboratories are generally well-resourced with the required equipment, and the whole experimental setting is supported by advanced computer and library services.

An alternative model is frequently implied in the literature in which the responsibility for discovery is attributed to the individual. This can be expressed as shown in Figure 12.

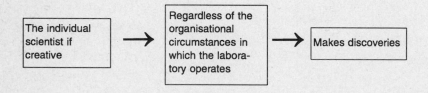

Figure 12 The implied model of discovery based in the individual

This view of discovery attributes the entire responsibility for successful research, to the individual scientist. The view seems to be that scientists, if highly creative, will overcome all obstacles placed in their way and reach successful conclusions. This ignores or at least minimises the effects of organisational circumstances as facilitators or inhibitors of the research process, and because it is not supported by the available evidence, is therefore rejected. The reader may think of individual scientists who have overcome great difficulties and reached major discoveries. This would seem to be more likely to occur in some fields of science such as mathematics or theoretical physics. However, though such examples do exist, they must be few indeed in such major areas of science as chemistry, biology, physics and medical research.

Some models of the process of research and discovery, such as those of Beveridge, Root-Bernstein, Conant, and Wallas, *imply* an organisational dimension, though this organisational dimension is not made explicit. Glueck and Thorpe (1971), however, do spell out an organisational model of the research process. This is given here as Figure 13.

This model describes the inputs to the process in terms of money, human resources and equipment; the organisational processes in terms of the environment, management, planning, coordination etc; and the outputs as new theories, ideas, solution to problems, and inventions. It regards the successful completion of good research as evidence of organisational effectiveness and health, and the lack of attainment of such goals as indicating the need for organisational change. This model is outlined in the introduction to a most useful annotated bibliography and synopsis of research related to the management of scientific research. It would now be timely to update this to take account of the work done in this area since 1971.

This is a useful model, but lacks two aspects of some importance. The first is an awareness that the selection of scientists is central to excellence in research. Scientists come in all sorts of personality types, some are more suited to the administration of existing projects, and the carrying out of prescribed tasks. Others are more suited to the uncertainty of speculative work.

The second aspect missing from this model is the extreme variation that exists in organisational terms. Very few research laboratories have that happy conjunction of favourable circumstances, including exceptional human and other resources, which seems to be so necessary for discovery to take place.

While we can see that these models do not provide us with an adequate explanation of the discovery process, they do contribute to our thinking, and stimulate us to develop a model which is specifically an organisational one — emphasising organisational processes — and which has as its outcome, discovery. Its inputs are those aspects of the individual scientist's personality, which are necessary for discovery to take place.

What we see emerging from the present study as our organisational model of the discovery process, is illustrated in the following figure. It is a process flow model, moving from the selection of a scientist, into the organisational processes which may affect that scientist. It has as its outcome, discovery. The model assumes the existence of a scientific organisation which has decided, presumably in relation to an experimental project to which it is committed, to select new discovery-oriented scientific people, and to organise itself in the best possible way.

Figure 14 may be read in the following way: individual characteristics are given as inputs to the scientific process; the scientist selected then enters a laboratory with certain organisational characteristics and processes; discovery is shown as a possible outcome on the right hand side. The vertical line of each triangle illustrates the 'domain of discourse'; the horizontal line of each triangle, the extent of the presence of each characteristic.

144

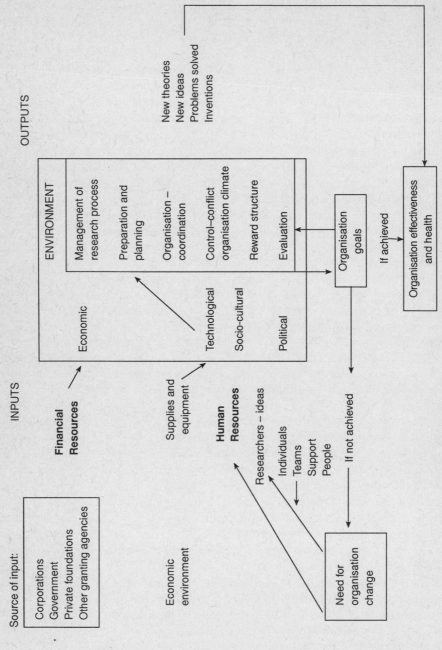

Figure 13 General model of the management of research (Glueck and Thorpe, 1971)

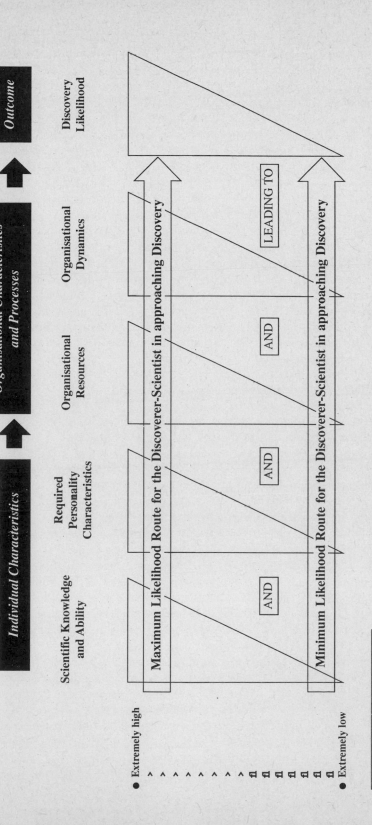

Figure 14 A proposed organisational model of discovery in science

In the processes outlined in this model, the organisation (laboratory, university, institute) selects a discovery-oriented scientist. This scientist is different from a 'science process' oriented scientist, who works within the existing frames of knowledge, and has little personal motivation to risk moving outside of them. The discovery-oriented scientist will have an exceptionally deep and broad knowledge and grounding in the chosen field of science (illustrated in the first triangle) and will have, to a high degree, personal characteristics such as persistence, curiosity and scientific motivation (illustrated in the second triangle). It is important that those deciding on the selection, should be clear that it is a discoverer-scientist they seek, not a scientist to teach, to administer or to control.

In joining a research-oriented laboratory scientists, as we have seen in Chapter 6, seem to be attracted to, or repelled by, those laboratories, depending on their personality characteristics. Those with both a compendious knowledge of their field, and unusually strong scientific curiosity, persistence and motivation, will be attracted by those research laboratories with researchers of international renown. Other scientists probably select themselves out of these laboratories in favour of those involved in less advanced research, or entirely out of research and into teaching, or scientific administration or monitoring. The particular scientist attracted to the discovery-oriented laboratory is probably in a small minority among the larger pool of scientists, who will correctly assess their own personal abilities, and work in areas which suit them.

These decisions—attraction by the scientist, acceptance by the laboratory—are central to the establishment of a pool of discovery-oriented scientists in any laboratory. However, the existence of attraction alone on the part of the scientist is no guarantee of discovery; the scientist may after all be incorrect in his or her self assessment. The organisation has a role to play in ensuring that the characteristics which a discovery-oriented laboratory requires, do not exist in high measure, in those they select.

Having selected the discoverer-scientist, that scientist enters an organisational system, in this case a laboratory. That laboratory is part of a larger organisation: a university, commercial laboratory, research institute or government service. The circumstances and dynamics of these laboratories wil be quite distinct. It is likely that the particular circumstances the scientist encounters will have strong effects on their performance, as we have seen in Chapter 5. The extent and nature of resource provision of the organisation is a key variable.

The well-resourced organisation (as we have seen in Chapter 3) provides the discoverer-scientist with a variety of important resources including equipment, technicians, research assistants, and the stimulation of talented colleagues (illustrated in the third triangle in Figure 14).

Next in the proposed model we see a range of organisational processes. The organisation provides a stable place to work, with that freedom the scientist needs, and a climate of enthusiasm and dedication. The organisation of the laboratory should, it is suggested, take an active role in developing techniques of problem-solving and idea generation in the discoverer-scientist (illustrated in the fourth triangle).

What is needed for discovery to be probable appears to be a unique combination of exceptional individual talent, with exceptional organisational resources and dynamics. The probability that discovery will occur depends on the extent of the required individual characteristics, coupled with extensive organisational resources and facilitating organisational processes (illustrated in the fifth triangle).

This model links individual and organisational aspects of the discovery process. It outlines the organisational processes in some detail, and gives little detail to the individual processes. This is not because individual factors are less important — clearly without individual talent discovery would not take place — but rather because individual factors alone do not provide a full explanation of discovery. In fact, part of the organisational process of research is to protect the individual scientist and to provide him or her with a climate of intellectual freedom essential to the work of science.

Of course we might say all research organisations have resources, colleagues, libraries, technical support and so on. But as we have seen in Chapter 2, the difference in scale between the level of resources of one university and another is so vast as to be different in kind, rather than quantity alone. In terms of financial resources, Stanford, for example, has 6.2 million books, another university of the same size in terms of students has 150 000. Stanford has a general budget of $1 200 000 000; another university of the same size in terms of student numbers, has $100 000 000.

We might also ask why does not every scientist who works in a highly resourced laboratory achieve distinctions such as the Nobel prize? Not every scientist in these universities has the unique set of personal characteristics to a high degree, which is so exceptional. Most scientists in such universities have selected themselves into taking different and valuable responsibilities for teaching, for administration, which effectively preclude exclusive concentration on research.

The 'route of maximum likelihood' in Figure 14 attempts to chart the progress of the scientist towards discovery. We cannot say in any deterministic way, that discovery will occur when the variables described exist to the greatest possible extent. Figure 14 is an attempt to illustrate in a probabilistic sense, that discovery is more likely to occur when high levels of these individual and organisational characteristics exist concurrently.

As far as can be determined, all sixteen Nobel laureates in this study have a compendious knowledge of their fields and of some others. They also have high levels of such individual characteristics as persistence, curiosity and scientific motivation. All of them worked in organisations from the time they had completed their doctoral studies, where the level of organisational resources was exceptionally high in both human and material senses. And we know that they have made substantial discoveries. This means that we have evidence to support the route described in Figure 14, as having the maximum likelihood of reaching discovery.

This does not mean that all those with low levels of persistence, curiosity, and other science related personality characteristics who enter organisations with low levels of resources and poor group dynamics, will not make discoveries, though it does suggest that in these cases, discovery is less likely to occur. Minimum likelihood routes to discovery are likely to be many and varied. The evidence suggests that those routes which lead to discovery with maximum likelihood are few, and defined in terms similar to those in Figure 14.

The nature of the required research

Of course the model presented in Figure 14 is essentially a speculation on the nature of reality. The research needed to establish the truth or falseness of this model is extensive, and it will also be varied, depending on which of the many facets of the problem is explored. An important starting point would be the development of agreed definitions of discovery, or of varying levels of discovery. The research will have a number of commonalities:

● It will be directed towards modelling the probability of scientific discovery in laboratories. This is in contrast to previous research which was directed either to creativity or to scientific *productivity*.
● It will be related to the organisational factors which impinge on discovery, including selection.
● It will be empirically based.
● It will be longitudinal, and will compare the effect over time, of the enhancement of organisational processes such as outlined in Chapter 6.
● It will require the active cooperation of scientists.
● For statistical reasons, measures will be required over a wide range of scientific quality.

Such research would be varied in its goals and methodologies. The possible goals for such research would include:

● exploring cognitive models of discovery in science;
● developing models of the organisational processes of assimilating, developing and training and supervising those involved in discovery;
● exploring more specific aspects, such as the selection and testing of discovery-oriented scientists; and
● identifying the structural aspects of the organisation in its relationship with research activity.

The embedding of creative functions within a large organisation, has a certain degree of irony attached to it. There is perhaps an essential conflict between the forces of stability and order, and the forces for new ideas, particularly discovery. Nevertheless, the discoverer-scientist as we have seen, does need stability and resource provision; the research laboratory has to exist within the larger, long-term structure. It may be that the research laboratory sits within the wider organisation at some remove.

In addition to research directed to answering questions of this kind, considerable work is also needed to develop an *agreed measure of discovery*. This is fundamental to research, as without it, we cannot be certain of our criterion.

In an ideal world, one could imagine a study involving the cooperation of, let us say, 60 university or commercial research laboratories. Each laboratory would be chosen as having broadly the same high level of organisational resources, and a generally poor record of significant scientific achievement. The set of laboratories would be randomly divided into two equal groups of 30 laboratories, one to be regarded as the control group in which nothing would change, the other the experimental. In the experimental group, each laboratory would be organisationally enriched in the following ways:

- An eminent scientist, such as a Nobel laureate in a related area, would join the reseach team.
- The principal investigator would receive organisational training and development would be provided, including leadership, management principles, etc.
- New research colleagues would be selected using professional recruitment people.
- Scientific problems would be addressed in the usual way, but would in addition be assisted by professionals running problem-solving procedures, such as Brainstorming; Synectics; de Bono technique etc.

A less ambitious experiment is also possible in which those laboratories where substantial discoveries have been made were studied in great detail to see if their individual and organisational characteristics and processes supported the hypothesis put forward here, namely that organisation — both as a noun and as a verb — is important in the discovery process. Conversely, laboratories of a similar size and in the same countries, but where no discovery of substance had been recorded, could be matched with the first group and compared in organisational terms.

To be accepted as valid, a model of discovery in science would need to use an agreed definition of scientific discovery; the factors involved, whether they be individual or environmental; the instruments to be used in as measures of discovery, and the method to be used to test the theory.

These are not minor issues; the most fundamental of these would appear to be the definition of discovery: is discovery a dichotomous phenomenon — either a discovery is made or not; or is it a variable ranging from very minor discoveries to outstandingly influential ones? Without an agreed defintion, it is difficult to conceive of a valid measure. Without a valid measure it is difficult to design a scientific exploration of those factors which may have a role in influencing the outcomes of successful research.

This is an exciting challenge for scientists and organisational thinkers alike. Scientists may have to consider their research in the light of its organisational dimension. What they see as the appropriate activities of research can be seen to have a strong organisational dimension. What the organisational thinker sees as the characteristics and processes of organisation can be seen to be, deeply and properly, the activities of the scientific researcher. Both fields have much to learn from one another.

The kind of organisation conceived here is well described by Conant as follows:

> There is only one proved method of assisting the advancement of pure science: that of picking men of genius, backing them heavily, and leaving them to direct themselves. James Bryant Conant (1945)

Conant elegantly expresses in this short sentence the need for those most central of organisational processes; in referring to 'picking men of genius' he refers to the need for valid methods of selection; in referring to 'backing them heavily' he means the provision of extensive organisational resources; and in speaking of 'leaving them to direct themselves' he refers to the need for the organisation and the laboratory to ensure free and autonomous working groups in research.

If the conceptualisation of the process of discovery given here is correct, it will come as no surprise that very talented individual scientists need to be identified and selected for discovery-related projects. Science without such exceptionally talented individuals is unlikely to progress to discovery. However, the development of expertise in this selection process may have to be accelerated. Also, a closer examination of the professional competencies — in addition to individual characteristics — is needed. We need to know the precise nature of the professional development of scientists which will equip them for the route towards discovery.

We need to know much more about how decisions are made by scientists; why one avenue of exploration is pursued, and not another. Also, we need to know much more about the effect of group discussion on thought development.

It will also come as no surprise that substantial resources are needed for discovery to thrive. What may not be so widely appreciated is that it is not simply extensive financial and physical resources that are required, but resources of a more organisationally dynamic kind, involving the active deployment of carefully thought out strategies and processes in laboratories which have been found to be useful in fostering discovery.

References

Albert, R. S. (1983). *Genius and Eminence*. Pergamon Press.

Albert, R. S., and Runco, M. A. (1989). Independence and the creative potential of gifted and exceptionally gifted boys, *Journal of Youth Adolescence*, June, **18**(3), 221–30.

Amabile, T. M. (1983). *The Social Psychology of Creativity*, Springer Verlag, New York.

Amabile, T. M. (1988). A model of creativity and innovation in organisations, in B. M. Staw, and L. Cummings (eds), *Research in Organisational Behaviour*, Greenwich.

Amabile, T. M. (1989). How work environments affect creativity, IEEE International Conference Proceedings on *Systems, Man and Cybernetics*, Vol. 1, pp. 50–55.

Amabile, T. M. (1993). What does a theory of creativity require? *Psychological Inquiry*, **4**(3), 179–81

Amabile, T. M., Goldfurb, P., and Brackfield, S. C. (1990). Social influences on creativity: evaluation, coaction and surveillance. *Research Journal*, **3**(1), 6–21.

Amabile, T. M., and Griskievicz, N. (1989). The creative environment scales, *Creativity Research Journal*, **2**, 231–53.

Andrews, F. M. (1967). Creative ability, the laboratory environment, and scientific performance, *IEEE Transactions on Engineering Management*, June, **14**(2), 76–83.

Andrews, F. M., and Gordon, G. (1970). Social and organizational factors affecting innovation in research, Proceedings of the Annual Convention of the American Psychological Association, Part 2, pp. 589–90.

Andrews, F. M. (1975). Social and psychological factors which influence the creative process, in I. A. Taylor and J. W. Getzels (eds.), *Perspectives in Creativity*, New York, Aldine, pp. 60–89.

Ashton, S. V., and Oppenheim, C. (1978). A method of predicting Nobel Prizewinners, *Chemistry Social Studies in Science*, **8**, 341–8.

Asimov, I. (1984). *Asimov's New Guide to Science*, Penguin, London.

Bacon, Francis (1605). *Advancement of Learning*, Book 1, Vol. VII, p. 5.

Bacon, F. (1620). *The Great Instauration*, Crofts Classics, Illinois (1989).

Bandura, A. (1977). Self-Efficacy: toward a unifying theory of behavioural change, *Psychological Review*, **84**, 191–215.

Bandura, A. (1986). *Social Foundations of Thought and Action*, Prentice Hall, Englewood Cliffs, New Jersey.

Bandura, A. (1991). Self-regulation of motivation through anticipatory and self-reactive mechanisms, in R. A. Dienstbier (ed.) Nebraska Symposium on *Motivation: Perspectives on Motivation, Current Theory and Research in Motivation*, Vol. 38, University of Nebraska Press, Lincoln, Nebraska.

Bargar, R. R, and Duncan, J. K. (1982). Cultivating creative endeavour in doctoral research, *Journal of Higher Education*, January–February, **53**(1), 1–31.

Barron, F., and Harrington, D. M. (1981). Creativity, intelligence and personality, *Annual Review of Psychology*, **32**, 439–76.

Bauer, H. (1992). *Scientific Literacy and the Myth of the Scientific Method*, University of Illinois Press, Chicago.

Benacerraf, B. (1985). Reminiscences. *Immunological Reviews*, **84** (July).

Benacerraf, B. (1991). When all is said and done. *Annual Review of Immunology*, **9**, 1–26.

Beveridge, W. I. B. (1950). *The Art of Scientific Investigation*, Heinemann, London.

Beveridge, W. I. B. (1980). *Seeds of Discovery*, W. W. Norton, New York.

Bland, C. J., and Ruffin, M. T. (1992). Characteristics of a productive research environment, *Academic Medicine*, **67**(6), 385–97.

Blumberg, B., Sutnick, A. I., London, W. T., and Millman, I. (1973). Australia antigen, in Edward Gall (ed.), *Liver*, pp. 269–85, Williams and Wilkins, Baltimore, Maryland.

Boxenbaum, Harold (1991). Scientific creativity: a review, *Drug Metabolism Reviews*, **23**(5 and 6), 473–92.

Brannigan, A. (1981). *The Social Basis of Scientific Discoveries*, Cambridge University Press.

Briggs, J. (1984). The genius mind, *Science Digest*, **92**, 75–79, 100–102.

Brown, H. C., and Rao, B. C. S. (1956). A new technique for the conversion of olefins into organoboranes and related alcohols, *Journal of the American Chemical Society*, **78**, 5694–5.

Butera, F. (1975). Environmental factors in job and organisation design: the case of Olivetti, in L. E. Davies and A. B. Cherns (eds.), *The Quality of Working Life*, Vol. 1, pp. 166–200.

Campbell, D. T. (1960). Blind variation and selective retention in creative thought as in other knowledge processes, *Psychological Review*, **67**, 380–400.

Cannon, W. B. (1939). The role of chance in discovery. *Scientific Monthly*, **50**, 204–9.

Chambers, J. A. (1969). Beginning a multidimensional theory of creativity, *Psychological Reports*, **25**, 779–99.

Clark, K. (1957). *America's Psychologists*. American Psychological Association, Washington, D.C.

Clement, J. (1988). Learning via model construction and criticism: protocol evidence on sources of creativity in science, Scientific Research Report, Massachusetts University, 17 December.

Cohen, B. P., Kruse, R. J., and Anbar, M. (1982). The social structure of research teams. *Pacific Sociological Review*, **25**, 205–32.

Cole, S., and Cole, J. R. (1967). Scientific output and recognition: a study in the operation of the reward system, *Sociological Review*, **32**, 377–90.

Cole, S., and Cole, J. R. (1973). *Social Stratification in Science*, University of Chicago Press.

Cole, S. (1979). Age and scientific performance, *American Journal of Sociology*, **84**, 958–77.

Conant, J. B. (1947). *On Understanding Science: An Historical Approach*, Yale University Press (SUL), New Haven, Connecticut.

Crane, D. (1965). Scientists at major and minor universities: a study of productivity and recognition, *American Sociological Review*, **30**, 669–714.

Csikszentmihalyi, M. (1988). Motivation and creativity ..., *New Ideas in Psychology*, **6**(2), 159–76.

Dale, B., and Cooper, C. (1992). *Total Quality and Human Resources: An Executive Guide*. Blackwell, London.

Damanpour, F. (1987). The adoption of technological, administrative and ancillary innovations, *Journal of Management*, **13**, 675–88.

Dasgupta, S. (1994). *Creativity in Invention and Design*, Cambridge UP, Cambridge.

Davis, L. E., and Cherns, A. B. (1975). *The Quality of Working Life*, Free Press, New York.

de Bono, E. (1971). *Lateral Thinking for Management*, McGraw-Hill, New York, p. 533.

De Charms, R. (1968). *Personal Causation*, Academic Press, New York.

Den Hertog, F. J. (1974). *Work Structuring*, Philips Gloeilampenfabrieken, Eindhoven, The Netherlands.

Dewey, John (1917). *Creative Intelligence*. Holt, New York.

Diderot, Denis (1753). *On the Interpretation of Nature*.

Drenth, P. (1989). Introduction, in P. Herriot (ed.), *Assessment and Selection in Organisations*, John Wiley, Chichester.

Eigen, Manfred (1991). *Jenseits von Ideologien und Wunschdenken*, Piper, Munich.

Einstein, A., and Infeld, L. (1938). *The Evolution of Physics*. Simon and Schuster, New York, p. 95.

Ekvall, G., and Tangeberg-Andersson, Y. (1986). Working climate and creativity: a study of an innovative newspaper office. *The Journal of Creative Behaviour*, **20**(3), 3rd Quarter, 215–24.

Elshout, J., Boselie, F., van den Berg, J., Boerlijst, G., and Schaake, B. (1973). De validatie van een testbatterij voor de selectie van wetenschappelijke onderzoekers, in P. Drenth, P. Williams and Ch. de Wolff (eds.), *Arbeids en Organisatiepsychologie*, Kluwer, Deventer.

Ericsson, K., Krampe, R., and Tesch-Romer, C. (1993). The role of deliberate practice in the acquisition of expert performance. *Psychological Review*, **100**(3), 363–406.

Feyerabend, P. (1970). Against method, *Minnesota Studies in the Philosophy of Science*, **IV**, 17–30.

Findlay, J. W. (1974). The 1974 Nobel Prize in Physics, *Science*, **186**, 620–1.

Findlay, C. and Lumsden, C. (1988). The creative mind, *Journal of Social and Biological Structures*, January, **11**(1), 3–55.

Frederiksen, N., and Ward, E. (1973). Development of provisional criteria for the study of scientific creativity, Educational Testing Service, February, 10 pages. Paper presented at Annual Meeting of American Educational Association, New Orleans, Louisiana, 25 February–March 1973, Vol. 1.

Galison, P. (1987). *How Experiments End*, Chicago: University of Chicago Press, Chicago.

Garfield, E. (1970). Citation indexing for studying science, *Nature*, **222**, 669–70.

Gist, M., and Mitchell, T. (1992). Self-efficacy: a theoretical analysis of its determinants and malleability. *Academy of Management Review*, April, 183–211

Glenn, N., and Villemez, N. (1970). The productivity of sociologists at 45 American universities, *American Sociologist*, **5**, 244–52.

Glover, J. A, Ronning, R., and Reynolds, C. R. (1989). *Handbook of Creativity*, Plenum Press, New York.

Glueck, W. and Thorpe, C. (1971). *The Management of Scientific Research*, University Missouri Press.

Glueck, W. F., and Jauch, L. R. (1975). Sources of research ideas among productive scholars, *Journal of Higher Education* (*JHE*), January–February, **XLVI**(1, 103), 104–14.

Gough, H. G. (1976). Studying creativity by means of word association tests, *Journal of Applied Psychology*, **61**, 348–53.

Gough, H. G. (1976). A new scientific uses test and its relationship to creativity in research, *Journal of Creative Behaviour*, **9**(9), 4th Quarter, 245–52.

Gould, S. J. (1996). Why Darwin?, *New York Review of Books*, 4 April 1996, 10–14.

Greene, J. E. (1980). *McGraw-Hill Modern Scientists and Engineers*, McGraw-Hill, New York.

Guilford, J. P. (1970). Creativity. *American Psychologist*, **5**, 444–54.

Guilford, J. P. (1967a). Creativity: yesterday, today, and tomorrow, *Journal of Creative Behaviour*, **1**(1), 3–14.

Guilford, J. P. (1967b) *The Nature of Human Intelligence*, McGraw-Hill, New York.

Guilford, J. P., *et al.* (1951–1956). University of Southern California Psychology Laboratory Reports: No. 4, 1951; No. 8, 1952; No. 11, 1954; No. 16, 1956.

Hadamard, J. (1988). How I did not discover relativity, *Mathematical Intelligencer*, **10**(2), 65–7.

Hannon, P. J., Rustum, R., and Christman, J. (1988). Chance and Nobel prize. *Chemtech*, October, pp. 594–98.

Harre, R. (1981). *Great Scientific Experiments*, Phaidon Press, Oxford.

Hayes, J. R. (1989). Cognitive processes in creativity, in J. A. Glover, R. Ronning, and C. R. Reynolds, (eds.), *Handbook of Creativity*, Plenum Press, New York.

Heckhausen, H. (1991). *Motivation and Action*, Springer Verlag, Berlin, p. 11.

Hegel, G. (1971). *Philosophy of Mind*, Vol. 10, No. 2, Clarendon Press, Oxford, pp. 65–7 (1988 reprint).

Herriot, P. (ed.) (1989). *Assessment and Selection in Organisations*, John Wiley, Chichester.

Hesse, M. B. (1963). *Models and Analogies in Science*, Sheed and Ward, London.

Hewish, A. (1968). Pulsars. *Scientific American*, **219**(4), 25–35.

Hitchings, G. H. (1989). Selective inhibitors of dihydrofolate reductase (Nobel Lecture in Physiology or Medicine 1988), *In Vitro Cellular and Developmental Biology*, April, **25**(4), 303–10.

Hocevar, D. (1980). Intelligence, divergent thinking, and creativity, *Intelligence*, **4**(1), 25–40.

Hocevar, D., and Bachelor, P. (1989). A taxonomy and critique of measurements used in the study of creativity, in J. A. Glover, R. Ronning and C. R. Reynolds (eds.), *Handbook of Creativity*, Plenum, New York.

Hoffman, E. P. (1994). The Evolving Genome Project: Current and Future Impact, *American Journal of Human Genetics*, **54**, 129–36.

Howard, A., and Bray, W. (1988). *Managerial Lives in Transition: Advancing Age and Changing Times*, Guilford Press, New York.

Hudson, L. (1966). *Contrary Imaginations*, Methuen, London.

Hurley, J. (1982). *Productivity, Organisation, and Employee Attitudes*. Doctoral Dissertation, University of Nijmegen, The Netherlands.

Hurley, J. (1990). The collaborative imperative of new technology organisations, *Irish Journal of Psychology*, **11**(2), 211–20.

Janis, I. L. (1982). *Groupthink*. 2nd ed., Boston, Houghton Mifflin.

Johnson-Laird, P. N. (1988). *The Computer and the Mind*, Fontana, London.

Kanter, S. H. (1984). An investigation of the concurrent validity of selected subtests of Torrance tests of creative thinking among individuals at high levels of recognition in art and science. *Dissertation Abstracts*, February, **44**(8-A).

Kantorovich, A. (1993). *Scientific Discovery*, State University of New York Press, Albany.

Kantorovich, A., and Ne'eman, Y. (1989). Serendipity as a source of evolutionary progress in science. *Studies in History of the Philosophy of Science*, **20**, 505.

Kephart, W. M. (1950). A quantitative analysis of intragroup relationships, *American Journal of Sociology*, **60**, 544–9.

Kisiel, T. (1983). Scientific discovery: the larger problem situation, *New Ideas in Psychology*, **1**(2), 99–109.

Kitcher, P. (1993). *The Advancement of Science*, Oxford University Press, Oxford.

Koestler, A. (1976). *The Act of Creation*, Hutchinson, London.

Kuhn, T. (1962). *The Structure of Scientific Revolutions*, University of Chicago Press, Chicago.

Lakatos, I. (1978). In J. Worrall and G. Currie (eds.), *The Methodology of Scientific Research Programmes*, Cambridge University Press, Cambridge.

Lamb, D. (1991). *Discovery, Creativity and Problem-solving*, Ashgate Publishing Co. UK.

Langley, P. (1987). *Scientific Discovery; Computational Explanations of the Creative Process*, MIT.

Latour, Bruno (1987). *Science in Action*, Harvard University Press, Cambridge, Massachusetts.

Lenox, R. S. (1985). Educating for serendipitous discovery, *Journal of Chemical Education*, **62**(4), 282–5

Leopold, Carl (1978). The act of creation..., *Bioscience*, **28**, 436–40.

Lindauer, M. S. (1977). Imagery from the point of view of psychological aesthetics, the arts, and creativity. *Journal of Mental Imagery*, **2**, 343–62

Lipetz, B.-A. (1965). *The Measurement of Efficiency of Scientific Research*, Intermedia, Inc., Carlisle, Massachusetts.

Locke, Edwin (1968). Towards a theory of task motivation and incentives, *Organisational Behaviour and Human Performance*, May, **3**(2).

Loehle, C. (1990). A guide to increased creativity in research inspiration or perspiration, *Bioscience (USA)*, February, **40**(2), 123–9.

Lonergan, B. (1957). *Insight*, Longmans, New York, p. 4.

Lorenz, K. M. (1977). The creative hypothesis and the teaching of science, *Dissertation Abstracts International*, February, **37**(8-A), 5015–16.

Lucretius, T. (1995). *On the Nature of Things*. (*De rerum natura*), Johns Hopkins University Press.

McGrayne, S. B. (1993). *Nobel Prize Women in Science*, Birch Lane Press, New York.

Mach, Ernst (1943). *Popular Scientific Lectures*, Open Court, La Salle, Illinois.

Machiavelli, N. (1513). *The Prince*, Oxford University Press, 1992, p. 21.

Mackay, A. L. (1991). *A Dictionary of Scientific Quotations*, with a foreword by Sir Peter Medawar, A. Hilger, Bristol, Philadelphia.

Mackay, A. (1992). *A Dictionary of Scientific Quotations*, Institute of Physics Publishing, Philadelphia.

MacKinnon, D. W. (1960). The high effective individual, *Teachers College Record*, **61**(7), 367–78.

MacKinnon, D. W. (1962). The nature and nurture of creative talent, *American Psychologist*, **17**, 484–95.

MacKinnon, D. W. (1975). IPAR's contribution to the conceptualisation and study of creativity, in I. A. Taylor and J. W. Getzels (eds.), *Perspectives in Creativity*, Aldine, New York, pp. 60-89.

Mansfield, R. S., and Busse, T. V. (1981). *The Psychology of Creativity and Discovery: Scientists and Their Work*, Nelson Hall Inc.

Maritain, J. (1954). *Creative Intuition in Art and Poetry*. Harvill Press, London.

Maslow, A. (1943). A theory of human motivation, *Psychological Review*, **50**, 372–96.

Medawar, Peter (1985). *The Limits of Science*, Oxford University Press, Oxford.

Mednick, S. A. (1962). The associative basis of the creative processes, *Psychological Review*, **69**, 220–32.

Mednick, M. T. (1963). Research creativity in psychology graduate students, *Journal of Consulting Psychology*, **27**, 265–6.

Merton, Robert (1973). *The Sociology of Science*, University of Chicago Press, Chicago.

Mullins, C. J. (1963). Prediction of creativity in a sample of research scientists, *IEEE Transactions on Engineering Management*, **10**, 52–7.

Newell, A., and Simon, H. (1972). *Human Problem-Solving*, Prentice-Hall, Englewood Cliffs, New Jersey.

Nickles, T. (1978). *Scientific Discovery: Logic and Rationality*, Bowker.

Park, K. (1984). Bacon's 'enchanted glass', *ISIS*, **75**, 290–302.

Parloff, M. B., Datta, L., Kleman, M., and Handlow, J. (1968). Personality characteristics which differentiate creative male adolescents and adults. *Journal of Personality*, **36**, 528–52.

Pelz, D. C., and Andrews, F. M. (1976). *Scientists in Organisations*, Institute for Social Research, University of Michigan Press, Ann Arbor (originally published by John Wiley in 1966).

Perkins, D. (1992). The topography of invention, in R. W. Weber and D. Perkins (eds.), *Inventive Minds*. Oxford University Press, Oxford.

Perutz, Max (1989). *Is Science Necessary?*, Oxford University Press, Oxford.

Polanyi, M. (1962). The republic of science, *Minerva*, **1**, 54–73.

Popper, K. R. (1958). *The Logic of Scientific Discovery*, Hutchinson, London.

Popper, K. R. (1959). *The Logic of Scientific Discovery*, Harper, New York.

Popper, K. R. (1963). *Conjectures and Refutations*, Routledge and Kegan Paul, London.

Porter, L. W., Lawler, E. E., and Hackman, J. R. (1975). *Behaviour in Organisations*, McGraw-Hill, New York.

Prentky, R. A. (1980). *Creativity and Psychopathology: A Neurocognitive Perspective*, Praeger, New York.

Prince, G. M. (1970). *Practice of Creativity*, Harper and Row, New York.

Prince, G. M. (1980). Creativity and learning as skills not talents, Reprinted from the June–July 1980 and September–October 1980 issues of the Phillips Exeter Bulletin.

Reiser, M. F. (1971). Psychological issues in training for research in psychiatry, *Journal of Psychiatric Research*, **8**, 531–7.

Roberts, R. (1989). *Serendipity. Accidental Discoveries in Science*, John Wiley, New York.

Robertson, T. Cooper, D., and Smith, M. (1992). *Motivation: Strategies, Theory and Practice*, Institute of Personnel Management, London.

Roe, Anne (1953). *The Making of a Scientist*. Dodd, Mead, New York.

Root-Bernstein, R. S. (1988). Setting the stage for discovery, *The Sciences*, May/June, 26–35.

Root-Bernstein, R. S. (1989). *Discovering*, Harvard University Press, Cambridge, Massachusetts.

Root-Bernstein, R. (1994). The discovery process, *Chemtech*, May, pp. 15–20.

Rosenfeld, R., and Servo, J. (1994). Facilitating innovation in large organisations, in M. West, and J. Farr (eds.), *Innovation and Creativity at Work*, John Wiley, Chichester, pp. 15–20.

Runco, M. A., and Albert, R. S. (1990). *Theories of Creativity*, Sage Newbury.

Runco, M. A., and Bahleda, M. D. (1986). Implicit theories of artistic scientific and everyday creativity, *Journal of Creative Behaviour*, **20**(2), 2nd Quarter, 93–8.

Ryhammar, L., and Brolin, C. (1991). Creativity in the university — is there a need for research? *Scandinavian Journal of Educational Research*, **35**, 269–85.

Schein, E. (1980). *Organisational Psychology*, Prentice-Hall, Englewood Cliffs, New Jersey.

Scott, A. (1990). *Frontiers of Science*, Blackwell, London.

Schlipp, P. A. (1951). *Albert Einstein*, Harper, New York.

Shapere, D. (1992). Meaning and Scientific Change, in I. Hacking (ed.), *Scientific Revolutions*, Oxford University Press, Oxford.

Shapin, S., and Schaffer, S. (1985). *Leviathan and the Air-Pump*, Princeton University Press, Princeton.

Shaw, M. P. (1989). The Eureka Process: a structure for the creative experience in science and engineering, *Creativity Research Journal*, 2(4), 286–98.

Shrager, J., and Langley, P. (1990). *Computational Models of Scientific Discovery and Theory Formation*, Morgan Kaufmann, California.

Simon, H. (1985). Psychology of scientific discovery, Paper presented to the 93rd Annual APA Meeting, Los Angeles, California, 1985; also in *Research*, 1991, 35(4).

Simonton, D. K. (1988a). Quality and purpose, quantity and chance. University California, Davis, *Creativity Research Journal*, December, 1, 68–74.

Simonton, D. K. (1988b). *Scientific Genius: A Psychology of Science*, Cambridge University Press, Cambridge.

Simonton, D. K. (1990). *Psychology, Science and History*, Yale University Press, New Haven, Connecticut.

Sindermann, C. (1985). *The Joy of Science*, Plenum Press, New York.

Smith, M., and Robertson, I. (1989). *Advances in Selection and Assessment*, John Wiley, Chichester.

Stemwedel, J. (1994). Personal notes to this author. Department of Philosophy, Stanford University.

Sternberg, R. J. (1988). *The Nature of Creativity*, Cambridge University Press, Cambridge.

Sternberg, R. L., and Lubart, T. I. (1992). The creative mind, *Nederlands a Tijdschrift voor de Psychologie*, 47, 288–300.

Sutton, Christine (1986). Serendipity or sound science?, *New Scientist*, 27 February 1986, 30–2.

Taylor, I. A., and Sandler, B. E. (1973). Developing creativity in research chemists, *Proceedings of the 81st Annual Convention of the American Psychological Association*, Montreal, Canada, 8, 587–8.

Taylor, I. A., and Getzels, J. W. (eds.), (1975). *Perspectives in Creativity*, Aldine, New York.

Torrance, E. P. (1974). *Torrance Tests of Creative Thinking: Norms*, Technical Manual, Bensenville, Illinois.

UNESCO (1993). *Statistical Yearbook*, Paris.

Vernon, P. E. (1967). Psychological studies of creativity, *Journal of Child Psychology and Psychiatry*, 8, 153–64.

Vroom, V. H. (1964). *Work and Motivation*, John Wiley, Chichester.

Waldrop, M. M. (1990). Physics Nobel honours discovery of Quarks, *Science*, 250, 508–9.

Wallas, G. (1926). *The Art of Thought*, Harcourt Brace, New York.

Watson, J. (1968). *The Double Helix*. Norton.

Weiner, B. (1985). An attribution theory of achievement motivation and emotion, *Psychological Review*, 92, 548–73.

Wells, W. P., and Pelz, D. (1976). Groups, Chapter 13, in D. D. Pelz and F. M. Andrews (eds.), *Scientists in Organisations*, Institute for Social Research, University of Michigan Press, Ann Arbor (originally published by John Wiley in 1966).

Wertheimer, M. (1945). *Productive Thinking*, Harper, New York.

West, M., and Farr, J. (1990). *Innovation and Creativity at Work*, John Wiley, Chichester.

Wilson, R. (1953). *Bibliography of Thinking, Including Creative Thinking, Reasoning, Evaluation and Planning*, Department of Psychology, USC.

Witt, L. A. (1992). Alienation among research scientists, *Journal of Social Psychology*, 133(2), 133–40.

Woodman, R. W., and Schoenfeldt, L. F. (1990). An interactionist model of creative behaviour, *Journal of Creative Behaviour*, 24(4), 279–90.

Worthley, J. (1992). Is science persistence a matter of values?, *Psychology of Women Quarterly*, **16**, 57–68.
Zaltman, G., Duncan, R., and Holbeck, J. (1973). *Innovations and Organisations*, Wiley, Chichester.
Zuckermann, H. (1967). Nobel Laureates in science. Patterns of productivity, collaboration and authorship, *American Sociological Review*, **32**, 391–402.
Zuckermann, Harriet (1977). *Scientific Elites*, Free Press, New York.

Appendix 1

Interview A

This was an 'EMIC' interview of an open nature. It started with a key question, and explored the key points made in response to that question in detail.

Interview with:

....

I'd like to focus in on the first time you had the feeling you were approaching something new in science; could you tell me about this?

(If off the point)—I am particularly interested in the organisational circumstances in which you worked.

Main points:
1

2

etc.

Tell me about 1

1.2

Tell me about 2

2.1

Tell me about 3

3.1

Appendix 2

Interview B

Structured Interview with:

....

How were you selected for your doctoral work?

How should people be selected for doctoral work?

Creativity stimulated first when?

Creativity stimulated by rivalry, competing with colleagues?

Importance of chance factors in your creative insights?

Importance of emotional, non-rational factors in your creative insights?

Creativity stimulated by examples in university?

What was it about the organisation of the project you felt encouraged creativity?

What in your undergraduate or postgraduate development stimulated your creativity?

In developing the beginnings of insights, did analogies from other unrelated areas help?

Do you think creative scientists should confine themselves to scientific creation, or join boards and committees?

What aspects of the organisation of a scientific project do you consider most important for creativity to be optimised?

Appendix 3

Questionnaires

This questionnaire included four main topics: selection experience of Nobel laureate; Nobel laureates' current selection practice; freedom; and chance.

Nobel Laureates' Own Selection Experience:

How were you selected for your first science job?

(Please describe here the selection process used and add extra pages if needed)

Specifically, what importance was attached by those selecting you, to the following selection procedures:
(scale 1–4: very important to very unimportant, 5 = never used) Please enter the number which corresponds most closely to your view.

1	2	3	4	5

The Interview

References

Their judgement of your previous work

The view of the search committee

The quality of your publications

The quantity of your publications

Evidence of very high ability
(e.g. GMAT, or SAT scores)

The results of specific tests of scientific
ability

The results of specific tests of scientific
creativity

The grade of your primary degree in
science

Your performance during a trial
period in their labortory

Your self-assessment

Your colleagues' assessment

Biographical data

A current supervisor's assessment

Your own future autobiography

Current Selection Practice

How do you select scientists for work in your laboratory?
(Please describe here your actual practice, add extra pages if needed)

Specifically, what importance do you attach to the following selection
procedures, some or all of which you may use:
(5 = very important, 1 = very unimportant, please enter the number which
corresponds most closely to your view)

1	2	3	4	5

The Interview

References

Your judgement of their previous work

The view of the search committee

The quality of their publications

The quantity of their publications

Evidence of very high ability
(e.g. GMAT, or SAT scores)

The results of specific tests of scientific
ability

The results of specific tests of scientific
creativity

The grade of their primary degree in
science

Their performance during a trial period
in your laboratory

Their self-assessment

Their colleagues' assessment

Biographical data

A current supervisor's assessment

Their own future autobiography

Freedom Questionnaire

		very unimportant	unimportant	important	very important
1	To be able to choose what I work on is				
2	To be free to make my own choices of problems is				

3 To use my own
judgement as to
what to work on is

4 Working as part of
a team is

5 Pressure from being
supervised is

6 Working within a
defined research
plan is

7 Pressure from peers is

8 Independence of
thought is

9 Freedom of thought is

	strongly disagree	disagree	agree	strongly agree

10 The frameworks of
existing science are
best guesses

11 The frameworks of
existing science are
precise uncontrovertible
descriptions

12 I have limited freedom
of choice

13 My work gives me
unexpected rewards

14 There is a positive
climate of innovation
in my research
laboratory

15 I work best under
constant pressure
of evaluation

16 There is a stimulating
physical ambience in
my research laboratory

17 There is scope for
playfulness in my work

18 There is security of
employment in my
work

Additional aspects:

Questionnaire: Chance

The 'Magical' view of chance:

How important have 'magical' chance factors been in your life generally?
(by 'magical' chance is meant some non-explainable haphazard occurrence
over which you have no control, such as your birth position in your family,
being born with a high IQ)
Write your view in here:

Please summarise your view on the following scale:
'Magical' chance factors in my life have been:
very unimportant   unimportant   important   very important
1   2   3   4
(circle one number)

How important have 'magical' chance factors been in relation to your creative
scientific discoveries?
(same definition as above)
Write your view in here:

Please summarise your view on the following scale:
'Magical' chance factors in my scientific discoveries have been:
very unimportant   unimportant   important   very important
1   2   3   4
(circle one number)

The cognitive view of chance:

How important have 'cognitive' chance factors been in your life?
(here chance is defined as the intersection of opportunity   with preparedness)
Write your view in here:

Please summarise your view on the following scale:
'cognitive' chance factors in my life have been:
very unimportant   unimportant   important   very important
1   2   3   4
(circle one number)

How important have 'cognitive' chance factors been in relation to your creative scientific discoveries?
(here chance is defined as the intersection of opportunity   with preparedness)
Write your view in here:

Please summarise your view on the following scale:
'Cognitive' chance factors in my scientific discoveries have been:
very unimportant   unimportant   important   very important
1   2   3   4
(circle one number)

Index

Index compiled by G. Jones